I0786253

ISBN-13:
978-1724736208

ISBN-10:
1724736205

DRAG411's Ten Black Books

Book 1:	**DRAG411's "DRAG Bully, A Survivor's Guide"**
	Copyright © 2015 and 2018
Book 2:	**DRAG411's "Original DRAG Handbook"**
	Copyright © 2010, 2011, 2012, 2014, and 2018
Book 3:	**DRAG411's "Crown Me! Winning Pageants"**
	Copyright © 2013, 2014, and 2018
Book 4:	**DRAG411's "DRAG King Guide"**
	Copyright © 2014 and 2018
Book 5:	**DRAG411's "DRAG Stories"**
	Copyright © 2011, 2014, and 2018
Book 6:	**DRAG411's "DRAG Mother, DRAG Father"**
	Copyright © 2012, 2014, and 2018
Book 7:	**DRAG411's "SPOTLIGHT TODAY"**
	Copyright © 2012 and 2018
Book 8:	**DRAG411's "DRAG Queen Guide"**
	Copyright © 2014 and 2018
Book 9:	Two Comedy Scripts:
	DRAG411's "Best Said Dead"
	Copyright © 2011, 2014, and 2018
	"Following Wynter"
	Copyright © 2012, 2014, and 2018
Book 10:	**DRAG411's "DRAG World"**
	Copyright © 2012 and 2018

From the best-selling author of "CommUnity of Transition,"
"Two Days Past Dead," The Novel and the sequel,
"Turn Around Bright Eyes, The DRAG Queen Killer,"
"Joey Brooks, The Show Must Go On,"
And "Waiting On God."

DRAG411's

DRAG Mother, DRAG Father
Honoring Mentors

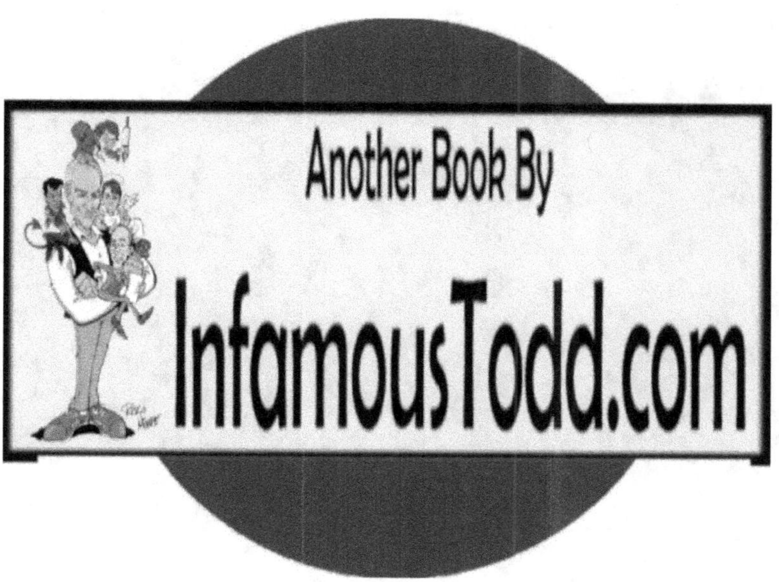

3rd Edition

I am not a fan of the term "drag" as applied across this entire art form, but until they find a single word "more accepting," I will have to use it. The drag community has helped me earn twenty LGBT world records. I created DRAG411 to document this form of entertainment. We are the world's largest organization for male, female, and androgynous impersonators with over 7,000 current or former impersonators in 32 countries.
                              The Infamous Todd Kachinski Kottmeier

(sic)

Latin adverb: thus"; in full: sic erat scriptum, thus was it written indicates DRAG411 transcribed the comments into this book exactly as found in the original source, complete with any erroneous or archaic spelling or other nonstandard presentation. We try to print the responses using the same words sent to us, ensuring the reader DRAG411 did not change the tone, reflection, or character of each response.

We print verbatim, without editing

ver·ba·tim   vər'bātəm/
adverb: verbatim; adjective
in exactly the same words as used originally.

Go to our website at
Drag411.com
to locate any name listed
in any of the books
in our Ten Black Book series
and the details of each
book, entertainer,
and chapter.

"Life is no brief candle for me.
It is a sort of splendid torch
which I have got hold of for
the moment and I want to
make it burn as brightly as
possible before handing it on
to future generations."

George Bernard Shaw

Another Record Breaking Book

The first book in history published to honor hundreds of mentors, created by incredible performers across the nation.

DRAG411's DRAG Memorial page on DRAG411.com

Dedication

The tree is the symbol of mentoring represented in this book project.

**"From the foundation of others,
you flourish;
From the work of others,
you thrive;
With the grace of your
environment,
you inspire."**

Todd Kachinski-Kottmeier

A tree is majestic in a forest, but has the ability to be strong standing by itself in a clear meadow.

We dedicate this book to those people that took time from their lives to touch our lives. We hope along the way, their stories will inspire you to be mentors of those seeking a hand to hold, a word to share, and a moment of your time.

This book we dedicate to the people creating your roots and the hopes of believing the best of them will inspire you to mentor someone with a positive light of growing the craft into the future.

"You need mentors, but in the end, you really need to just believe in yourself."
Diana Ross

And Contributing Writers

---

*We thank the following people
for being part of this groundbreaking project.*

Taina Norell
6pak
Bob Taylor
Horchata
Apple Love
Patricia Grand
Alexis Glasscock
Bunny Lee Pearson
Matthew Wolfe
Trinity Taylor
Domunique Jazmin Vizcaya
Brittany Moore
Shelita Taylor
Christopher Todd Guy
Adriana Manchez
Miml Welch
China Taylor
Armondis Bone't
Jake Lickus
Monique Trudeau
Simeon Codfish
AJ Menendez
Jerri Lynn
Diamond Dupree
Stefon Royce Iman
Jayden St James
Demonica da Bomb
Mr. Colin Grey
Teresa LeCroix
Mis Sadistic
Celyndra Clyne
Candice St. James
Alexis Glasscock
Justin Barnes Williams
Ivanna Dooche
London Taylor Douglas
Christina Alexandria Victoria Regina Lowe
Bianca DeMone
Critiqa Mann
PurrZsa Kyttyn
Jazmen Andrews
AJ Allen

TotiYanah Diamond
Gianna Love
D' Marco Knight
Chip Matthews
Mirage Montrese
India Starr Simms
Jade S. Stratton
Emerald Divine
Elysse Giovanni
David Warner
Vanity Halston
Kristofer Reynolds
Vinnie Marconi
Akasha Uravitch
Adriana Fuentes
Erykah Mirage
Raymond Jennewein
Felicity Ferraro
Vicious Slick
Joey Payge
Rhiannon Todd
Amirage Saling
TorI Sass
Chy'enne Valentino
Robbi Lynn
Naomi Wynters
Madisyn Michaels
Misty Eyez
Jocelyn Summers
Maxine Padlock
Kori Stevens
Stephen Brooks
Lona Honey
Ororo Summers
Lady Tajma Hall
Joey Brooks
Champagne T. Bordeaux
Deva DaVyne
Jade Shanell
Anastaio Fallon
Vivika D'Angelo
Rhyana Vorhman
Shugah Caine
Melissa Morgan
Miss Gigi
Amanda Love
Ada Buffet
Amy DeMilo
Tiffani Middlesexx
Coco Montrese
Pandora DeStrange

Michelle Tatum
Naomi D-Lish
Katrina Starr
Barbra Herr
Wendy G. Kennedy
Selina Kyle
Beverly LaSalle
Conundrum
Tabatha Lovall
LeeAnna Love
Ginger Minj
Adora
Dmentia Divinyl
Mr. Kenneth Blake
Esme Russell
Rusti Fawcett
Eunyce Raye
Danika Fierecë
ShaeShae LaReese
LaKeisha Pryce
Monique Michaels
Anastasia Rexia
Glitz Glam
Teri Courtney (RIP)
Nairobi D'Viante
Jade Jolie
Stephen Brooks
BukkakeBlaque London St James
Barbra Herr
Kiki LaFlare Santangilo
Ricki Lee
Patrice Knight
Twat Sisters
Raven Manniac
Stephen Brooks
Raquel Payne
Trixie LaRue
Jade Daniels
Kitty D'Meaner
Wendal Duppert
Aurora Sexton
Dmentia Divinyl
Lacy Lynn Taylor
Barbra Seville
Curtis Vegas Wixey
Jaeda Fuentes
Curtis Vegas Wixey
Barbra Seville

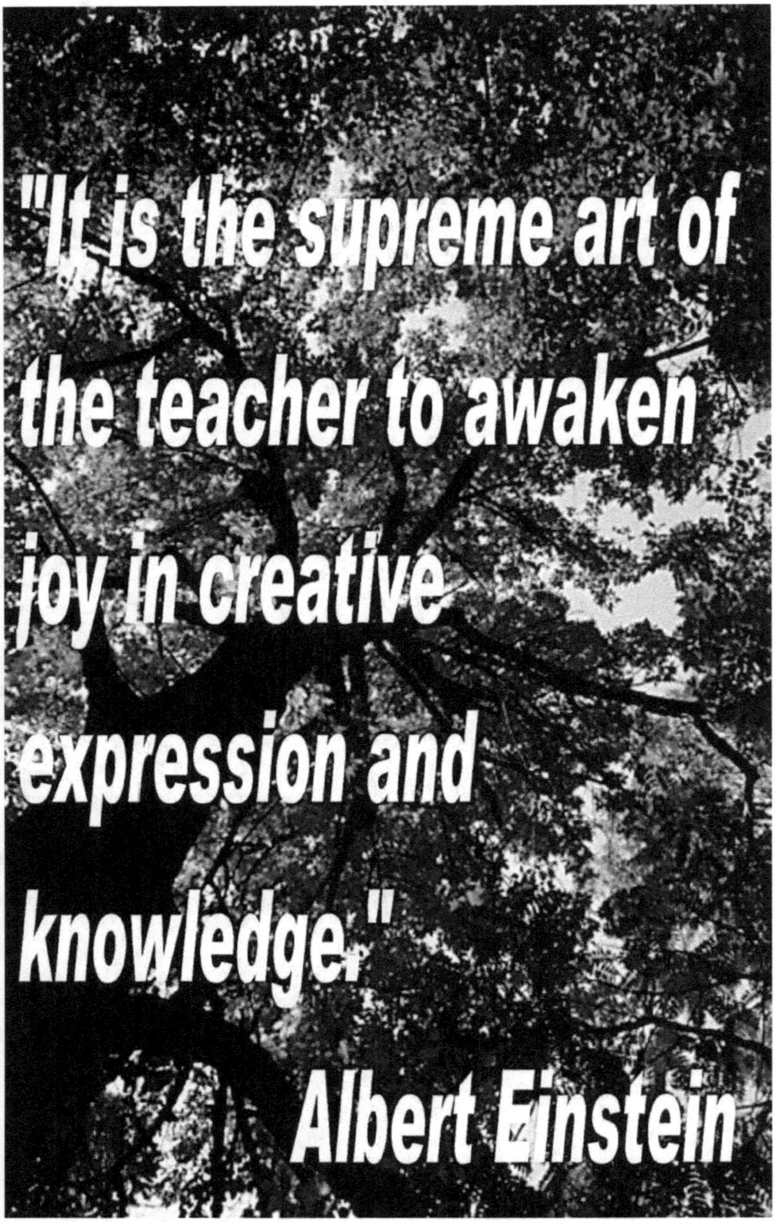

"It is the supreme art of the teacher to awaken joy in creative expression and knowledge."

Albert Einstein

Saluting

**Erika Norell
And Bob Taylor**

❀❀❀ *with limited editing* ❀❀❀

The talented diva Erika Norell took me under her wing many years ago. Erika is a loving mother giving me tough love, and taught me to have a backbone. She has been there through both the good and rough times of my life, and correctly played her role as my mother. Erika's word you could count on.

The first time I met Erika, she picked me up from my uncle's house in Miami. I was super nervous to meet such a talented diva, Miss Continental and Miss Gay USofA. I knew right from the start, I wanted her as my DRAG mother; she's Cuban like me!

I performed at the Voodoo Lounge that evening as Taina Tyler, and later in the night, I used the name Taina Norell honoring my DRAG mother. From that moment on, Norell became my name. I treasure my mother and adore her very much. She has so many sickeningly great qualities. She is not just my DRAG mother, but also my role model.

My DRAG father is Bob Taylor. This man came into my life and changed my attitude. Some DRAG queens get misled, letting the spotlight get to their heads. Bob brought me down to earth. He constantly gives me good advice and is always available to listen to me.

My genetic mother had my brother and me at a young age. My real father left us at a very early age, so I grew up having a father figure. Bob has done an amazing job filling that empty space inside of me.

We left the Honey Pot Night Club in Tampa one night after one of my shows. Back then, I didn't own a vehicle, so I needed a ride from Father Taylor. Suddenly Bob turned on a street that actually turned out to be the railroad tracks. I started screaming hysterically.

From the top of my lungs, I yelled "Railroad tracks, railroad tracks," Later it was hilarious. Moments you never forget. I am proud to say that I love both my parents; they both played an important role in my life.

Taina Norell

Unedited excerpts from the files of the
Number one selling book on this craft,

❀ Original DRAG Handbook ❀

These messages were shared in the questionnaire posted to create the book's vibe, content, and character. Pardon the English. Many confessed later that they filled out the forms after returning from the bars.

Naomi Wynters

I say people helped me succeed. I've always been told if you're not for me, you're against me... to a stance that's true. When you take that negativity and fuel it for your growth your purpose you succeed you have a fire and people do help me succeed because of so.

Madisyn Michaels

I take everyone's advice to heart, both good and bad. It builds your character and drives you to go above and beyond...

Misty Eyez

I have to thank Carlos and Stanley of Trixie's, Toni Barone of Elements, Howard Andrew, Jason Charles of Circuit, Eric Herb of Poplife Designs, DJ MiiK, I'd like to thank STEEL, Chris and Russell, Everyone at LIPS, Bills Filling Station Jackson and Mark and Jeff.... I'm not sure this is really that question so I will cut the list there, but it is a long list.

Saluting

Candi Stratton

❀❀❀ *with limited editing* ❀❀❀

My stage name was 6pak. I am now retired.

I had been in the industry for eight years when my DRAG Mom came into my life. In the beginning, I had much help from many of the entertainers. I had some ask to be my DRAG Mom, for me it was important to find someone to not only guide me but understand me, relate to me, and to be 100% honest with me.

Strange how it finally happened. My Wife Sasha and I had moved out to Vegas in 2009. By 2010, we knew we were moving back to Florida and got involved with the FTM Fund (renamed the Florida Trans Medical Fund).

We are the event/fundraising persons for the grant program. For our first annual fundraiser we put together a Trans Man Calendar and put a DRAG show together at Georgie's Alibi. We wanted to bring in some "Headliners" for the event as well. The first was Miss Conception from California.

The second person was Candi Stanton. We are very good friends with her though we never even met. I knew many things about her from watching video and television interviews she had done.I wrote her about our organization and the event hoping she would like to be a part of it. She responded immediately with her contact phone number. I can't remember what day I called Candi Stratton. I remember every word of our 2 ½ hour conversation (spending only ten minutes talking about the event).\

I had never felt a connection to anyone like I did with Candi. We shared many of the same thoughts, experiences, challenges, love for performing, and triumphs. Towards the end of the phone call, Candi asked unexpectedly, "Do you want me to be your DRAG Mom?"

Without skipping a beat, I replied "Yes!"

That was the day 6pak became Andrew Stratton. Candi Stratton has been everything a Mom should be; always there to listen, give advice, root for me and my wife, and tells me how proud she is of me.

Candi also keeps me grounded. She is always honest with me even when the truth hurts. I look up to her with respect, love, and gratitude... knowing I have the greatest DRAG Mom in the world!

Andrew Stratton aka 6pak

❀ Original DRAG Handbook ❀

These messages were shared in the questionnaire posted to create the book's vibe, content, and character. Pardon the English. Many confessed later that they filled out the forms after returning from the bars.

Teri Courtney (RIP)

My supporters have been mostly friends and fans.

Pandora DeStrange

It takes a village to raise a queen!

Saluting

**Tiffani Middlesexx,
Tina Devore, and
Candi Stratton**

❀❀❀ with limited editing ❀❀❀

I was nineteen enrolled at the University of Florida. I moved to Lakeland to drive back and forth allowing me to work locally. One night when my friend and I went to Tampa, we decided to go to the legendary Rene's Lounge on Kennedy Blvd.

We drank a lot that night as I cut the rug with my shirt off on the dance floor. Tiffani Middlesexx stopped to ask me if I could do choreography.

Of course, I said "Yes!"

The next day she had me back rehearsing and learning "Sweet Georgia Brown," a production for that upcoming weekend.

This is literally how Bob Taylor, the entertainer came to be. After that weekend, Middlesexx offered me a position as a male lead and dancer and I took it!

Over the next few years, Middlesexx would teach me about professional behavior, how to produce, choreograph, and teach. My life would never have gone in this direction had Middlesexx not come up to me on a whim that night.

I am so grateful Tiffani taught and mentored me, for she was truly one of the best. Tiffani is the reason I am intolerable of queens not wearing nails. I lived with Tiff for a few years (off and on) during the eighties and nineties. I was so lucky to watch and learn from her.

When the advertising company in Tampa promoted me after graduating college, they transferred me to Atlanta. I found the showplace for female impersonation on my second day there.

Lavita's was a magical place. Five nights a week the place was packed. I walked up to Tina Devore to introduce myself as a male lead and a titleholder from Tampa. I told her I wanted to be in her show. She smiled politely, most likely laughing under her breath. She explained they would have auditions soon.

Auditions were a month later. They hired me on the spot. Over time, I literally fell in love with the way Tina handled herself. She taught me so many things about being a fair person and treating others as you would want to be treated.

Over years, we grew closer and closer. Tina spent so many countless hours "grooming" me to be the person that I was meant to be, to become a teacher, a believer in dreams. Because of Tiffani and Tina, I am blessed to help many people in this art form. I am a better man because of these amazing human beings.

Candi was the first transsexual that I met face to face; that I had no idea was born a male. I was completely enthralled with her at the Miss Florida FI Pageant back in the eighties. After many years of knowing Candi, she adopted me two years ago to be her DRAG Son. She taught me that having more than one DRAG Mom is okay. I gain so much from all three of these remarkable people and if not for any of them, I would not be where I am today. I owe so much to Tiffani, Tina, and Candi and I sincerely hope that I have made them proud!

Bob Taylor

Saluting

Jennifer Warner

❀❀❀ *with limited editing* ❀❀❀

Dear Jennifer,

Assisting you for a year, I watched each night as you entertained. You always made me miss my days on the stage. I would see impersonators, and dancers, and often wonder why there was no representation of live singers.

Approaching the annual Independence Day show, I thought, "This is my chance to get in a show, let's see if we can add one more bit of variety to the stage. "

I nervously approached you with the idea. Our friendship had grown to be very near and dear, but you had never heard me sing.

Your response,"You're going to have to audition for me."

I stood and began to belt out the National Anthem with all my might. When I completed the song, you agreed to add me to the show, only after warning me that the audience was going to have an odd reaction to a live singer in a DRAG show.

It is our parents teaching us the lessons of life the "secrets" to help us get by. This is exactly what you did for me.

You told me, "Always keep them surprised and give them something fresh. Just because you sing, does not mean that you go out and just sing. Change your outfits, work the stage, and sing to your audience not just for them. "

You also warned me never to let them get me down no matter how much they may not pay attention. You told me to make them pay attention.

Give them all you've got and leave your heart out there with every performance.

I may have been the one out on the stage singing, but it was you giving me the chance to be there. Along with that chance, the first time you introduced me to the stage, you made me a part of your entertaining family and asked the crowd to "Welcome to the stage, the live vocal talents of David Warner."

From that night on you included me in so many shows and made me part of the cast in your monthly shows. The more I got exposure, the more I was liked, and this began to build a following.

Even though we were in two different fields of entertaining, I found myself watching you and learning the way you did things. I saw first-hand not only how successfully you were, but how respected you were throughout our community.

That is how I want to be, how I wanted to looked at. Just like with our parents and always wanting to make them proud, that is what I strived for with each performance because it is pride that I feel every time I they introduce me on stage as David Warner.

Thank you for the chance, for believing in me, for supporting me, and for always offering me your guidance. From friendship to Family, you have always been there for me and I am eternally grateful!

With all my love, your "Son in Song,"

David Warner

Saluting

Joe Romero

❀ ❀ ❀ with limited editing ❀ ❀ ❀

I never really had an upbringing by any performer that I did not see on television or in movies to show me what to do or how to be a performer. It was just fun, it was not until I met Joe Romero.

He was just a ball of glitter and "like a moth to flame" I was just in awe of the attraction he could produce. He could make anyone laugh, have fun, and enjoy being around him. I admired that his character became part of me. He was one of my closest friends and someone there when I was down or felt ugly.

My DRAG was not born from him, but he in his own way, guided me in the right direction. Well, I should not say right direction, but in a different direction.

I owe much of my DRAG persona to him. Always laughing, always having fun, and always, always feel fuckin' fabulous, no matter where I am. In memory of Joe Romero.

Horchata

"In the practice of tolerance, one's enemy is the best teacher. "

Dalai Lama

Saluting

Apple Love

❀❀❀ *with limited editing* ❀❀❀

It would be hard for me to begin to describe my relationship with my DRAG Mother without first giving the magical story in which Apple and I met. It was 2002 and I was 16 years old, and I was at a fabulous concert for Tori Amos at the Tampa Performing Arts Center.

I was a transgender teenager, not living full time. I went out as a girl or "in DRAG" any chance I could get, most especially occasions like concerts. I was there with a girl friend of mine, Lindsay that I met while attending Baptist school. My biological mother sent me to their school in an attempt to cure me of the demons of homosexuality (I came out to her 3 years previous).

Lindsay and I had artsy eccentricity along with being outcasts. There we were in the balcony, dressed to the nines in our freakish punky-goth-glam outfits, perched to watch Tori Amos pour her heart out on stage. Strangely enough, it was another red haired woman that captivated my attention that night: Apple Love.

Sitting a few rows from the front, was a beautiful woman on her feet with braids of red hair, wearing only black, raising her hands swaying to the melodious sound of Tori Amos and her piano.

Nothing seemed too unordinary about her, nothing that would have necessarily made me notice her any more than any other woman. Interestingly enough, I never read her as transgender. It was her magical glow and presence that exuded from her, that caught my attention more than the musical genius playing on center stage did.

I remember pointing her out to Lindsay and saying "There's something about this woman." I felt deep within my knowing body that this woman had some sort of power or something to her that was unlike most anyone else I've ever met.

I went home that night, lit some candles on my shrine to honor the beautiful experience of the evening, and went to sleep. I didn't give it much thought for the next couple of years.

Two years later it was my eighteenth birthday. I had decided a month or so before to begin taking hormones and living daily as who I felt I was and who I wanted to be. Friends and family deserted me for being transgender so I was spending my birthday alone. I went to Valentine's nightclub down the street from my house.

They announced "Apple Love," and out came this very beautiful woman limping for some reason beyond my comprehension.

I am a most certain that the song she was performing that night was Tori Amos, and as she commanded the stage from the center, the spotlight illuminating her sparkling frame, it seemed to me as though some Goddess, not from another world, but from the Earth, had appeared before me.

My body flooded with love and bliss. I began weeping, as though I was in some state of ecstasy. As the song ended, I fumbled for some crumpled dollars tucked in my purse and made my way up to tip her. She saw my tears, and drew me close to her. For a moment that seemed like an eternity. I felt safe and free of all the pain I was carrying from all the years of being ostracized, ridiculed, family disapproval, and harassment.

After the show, I introduced myself. Apple seemed a little astonished by my emotional state along with my reaction to her.

For the next few months, I started spending time with her getting to know her. At first, she was a bit reluctant to take me totally under her wing or call me her daughter. One evening, during the holidays we were touring the neighborhoods in her car looking at Christmas lights, and something jolted me. I looked at her and I was quiet for a moment.

I realized I have known this woman before I met her; this was the enchanting person from the concert. I felt tears well up in my eyes. I told her about Tori, I told her what she was wearing, I told her where she was sitting, I told her everything, and she looked at me as though she had seen a ghost.

We commented about how interesting and strange that was and carried on. As we grew together, we realized we had many things in common, such as interest in dark and beautiful music, alternative sub-cultures. We shared a particular aesthetic that is well beyond the surface, a kind of deep, dark beauty that encompasses and enchants.

The interesting thing about DRAG parents, is that in some cultures that have far more ancient subcultures of gender variant people, such as the Hijra of India (their third gender), is that they too have mothers, sisters, aunts or what we would consider "DRAG" family.

They also have spiritual framework and beliefs about these kinds of interactions and relationships. The Hijra believe that a soul is incarnated at least six times as a third gender person and that some of the older souls serve as gurus and mentors to the younger ones.

I don't know that I believe in afterlives or souls, but what I believe isn't as important as recognizing the magic and significance of my interaction with my DRAG mother. I know beyond any doubt that Apple and I share a connection that is unique, rare, and powerful.

Apple Love is very much like a mother to me, and a guru as well. She has guided me and been there for me in some of my most challenging and difficult times, and to celebrate many of my triumphs as well.

When my own family wasn't there for me, when I was called demon possessed for my gender and sexuality, and my chosen beliefs/disbelief by my biological mother who was raised Pentecostal, and called disgusting my hyper-masculine Latin father, she was there.

Living up to her namesake, Apple Love has shown me the kind of love and support I never found anywhere else. She grew up queer, gender variant, doing DRAG, while transitioning in a time that was far less accepting. Apple survived and thrived during a time when a person could be arrested for being openly LGBTQ or in DRAG. She succeeded beyond her polio, beyond her share of struggles and challenges which has made her one of the strongest and wisest people I have ever met.

Unlike many other performers, I have never once known her to be hateful to another person. When someone in a DRAG bar just starting and hasn't quite found their style or become comfortable in their skin, she shows them warmth and respect. On many occasions, when people are being hateful and disrespectful to another person, she fiercely calls them out. She points out that all of us in the community have been ridiculed for who we are and who we want to be. It is amazing to witness someone who is so beautiful outside to be as incredible inside.

I am now twenty-five, and have seen and done things I have experienced challenges and gone through struggles many people my age may have not. I have been to hell and back struggling to come into myself, and remove the fear and hatred instilled in me by Christian spirituality and religious abuse as a child.

I have overcome addictions and challenges, and through all of it, I know her love carries me on many occasions. Aside from helping me evolve into the artistic and dark stage personality that I now am Apple has guided me in ways that goes so much further than the stage.

When I finally matured and healed, it was very important to me to hear her call me "her daughter" and tell me she was proud of me.

Apple and I have never had one serious quarrel, aside from heated intellectual debates often ending in a loving respect and growth. She is one of the few people in the world I can totally be myself, no matter how bizarre and expressive I may be feeling.

I will proudly be Apple's DRAG daughter as I continue to grow with her until the day I die. If the beliefs of the Hijra are true, maybe we will see each other again in another life, in another world. For the time being, whatever may be true of gender variant people, and life and existence, I know that my relationship with my DRAG mother is one of my most precious relationships in life. I hold it to be sacred, and that I honor and love her deep within my heart.

As a side note, I would like to include that not all Hijra believe the same thing, or necessarily have religious beliefs, and that their community is very large and diverse. I do not want to speak on behalf of their entire population as far as what they believe, only include one possible dominant belief that I am aware of through my studies.

Gianna Love

"Experience is the teacher of all things."

Julius Caesar

Saluting

Dee Dee Williams

❀❀❀ *with limited editing* ❀❀❀

I remember like it was yesterday, the year was 1981 in Gainesville, Florida. I was walking in front of a club called the Spectrum when a large woman, who sounded like a man, walked up to me and asked me, did I know where I was?

I knew I wanted to join in the party in the club. Her name was Dee Dee Williams. She was so funny. We became the best of friends. I was very young and she told me the best way to get inside the clubs was to do DRAG.

Dee Dee painted my face and put me in a talent show at another club called The Melody Club. After I won, I was hooked. My DRAG mother shared the world through her eye and woke me up to all the things I should know. I don't think I would be around today without life lessons she taught me. Thank you mother Williams

Bunny Lee Pearson

Unedited excerpts from the files of the

Number one selling book on this craft,

❀ Original DRAG Handbook ❀

These messages are shared in the questionnaire posted to create the book's vibe, content, and character. Pardon the English. Many confessed later that they filled out the forms after returning from the bars.

Kori Stevens

Nobody is an island...whether people are for you or against you - they help make you who you are...it is that simple.

Adora

My first chance was given to me by Gary Santis at Warsaw South Beach , Then my first host job was at Barrio the legendary drag restaurant in South Beach , Twist in South Beach The Kremlin also South Beach there where very nice to me and because of their trust I think it help me , also my talent and hard work.

Dmentia Divinyl

I would like to say thank you to anyone who knows me personally regardless if I was your friend or enemy for giving me the reason to choose life over death and for making me the fierce diva and unstoppable energy that I am today.

Mr. Kenneth Blake

If it were not for the support of the audiences and the other entertainers, we encounter and learn from along the way; we would still be stuck lip-syncing to a Dianna Ross record in our bathroom mirror, with a towel on our head and a hairbrush in our hand.

Saluting

Leslie Elizabeth Lain,
Veronica Ciccione, and Jessica Ray

❀❀❀ *with limited editing* ❀❀❀

In 1998, I moved to Myrtle Beach, South Carolina from New York City. You have to believe that was a culture shock. However, the DRAG community reached out to me and was very generous. First, there was Leslie Elizabeth Lain, the Mouth of the South. I sat alone in the bar where she was show director. No one attempted to say hello. Leslie saw this, came over to me, and decided it was her job to introduce me to everyone in the bar. Each time I was there, she was very generous with her time and in fact, she booked me for her show, which began my performing career in Myrtle Beach.

The second DRAG queen who came to my aide was Veronica Ciccione. She noticed I had great difficulty with my makeup. Even my eyes would not cooperate. She volunteered to paint my face and that began a friendship. When I moved to Las Vegas, I invited her to join me partially because we were friends and partially because she made me look terrific. We continued living and working together in Las Vegas. Unfortunately, due to a family commitment, I had to move to Florida and Veronica moved home to North Carolina.

The third DRAG queen is Jessica Raye. She remains a friend until today. I could turn to her for bookings, combing out my wigs and anything else needed to perform. One night I went to her house to have my face painted. As I left her home, I drove into a ditch. There I was partially in DRAG and partially out. Her husband, Nick tried pulling my car out from the ditch but was unable. I called a tow truck. The driver arrived, walked up to my car. Suddenly he became very confused and could not decide to call me "Ma'am or sir." I enjoyed his confusion.

Patricia Grand

 Original DRAG Handbook 

These messages were shared in the questionnaire posted to create the book's vibe, content, and character. Pardon the English. Many confessed later that they filled out the forms after returning from the bars.

Tiffani Middlesexx

<Tiffani loves to write in all caps.> I HAVE BEEN SO FORTUNATE IN MY CAREER AS WELL AS IN LIFE TO HAVE BEEN ENCOURAGED AND SOMETIMES FINANCIALLY AIDED IN MY QUEST TO BE THE BEST IN WHAT TRUE FEMALE IMPERSONATION REALLY IS. IT CHANGED SO MUCH OVER THE YEARS AND NOT ALWAYS FOR THE BETTER.

Saluting

Morgan St. Clair
And Tara Williams

❀❀❀ *with limited editing* ❀❀❀

I am one lucky girl when it comes to DRAG mothers. I have two different mothers. My first DRAG mother instilled into me the excitement and wonder of female impersonation, her name was Morgan St. Clair. While she is no longer with us, she is with me. Her spirit encourages me to be the best I can be, and every time I put on an eyelash or a nail, I remember her. I remember her look the first time I slipped on a heel.

After Morgan's unexpected passing, I was lucky enough to be adopted by her best friend Tara Williams. Tara has taken me to places I never imagined I would be, from learning the basics of female impersonation to how to be a royal queen.

I never realized what it took to be a true professional. She taught me that a professional is not only on point while on stage, but even out of makeup and panty hose. You represent the best in the world of female impersonation through all you do.

I remember my first pageant; it was tragic, but she was there with me saying, "Did you do your best? If you did your best, be proud!"

Talk about encouragement!

The night I won my first crown, she did the most special thing for me. Tara heard I won the pageant before it was announced. She went and got a crown previously worn by Morgan St. Clair, my first DRAG mother. She made sure that I was crowned with it.

I was not only being honored for my hard work that night but she reminded me that I have a very special mother looking down on me; she would have been so proud. I know I would never be who I am now without these two wonderful women in my life. Thank you Morgan and Tara, you have truly taught me so much and taken me and our art to a much higher level!

Alexis Glasscock

"I am indebted to my father for living, but to my teacher for living well."

Alexander the Great

Unedited excerpts from the files of the
Number one selling book on this craft,

❀ Original DRAG Handbook ❀

These messages were shared in the questionnaire posted to create the book's vibe, content, and character. Pardon the English. Many confessed later that they filled out the forms after returning from the bars.

Jade Shanell

I have my husband and family and friends helping me become the queen I am. My husband "Shawna Roze" for showing me the trick of the trades, My parents for being so supportive and friends being so supportive and being my biggest fans.

Anastasia Fallon

I'm a lucky one, but I've always been shown tons of love and support throughout my career. There have been some bumps in the road, and performers I didn't particularly care for, but overall, the sense of community I got from my experience is irreplaceable...and the love from my biological family has brought me to tears at times. I know that people have my back no matter what, and to the negative people.

Vivika D'Angelo

It all falls on my family and friends and the venues I perform at without them I would not be me.

Lona Honey

Nobody can give you your talent, creativity, or drive most of all. But in my opinion we all have had someone put an opportunity in front of us that has made us prosper. Without these 'foot in the door' opportunities, I don't think any entertainer would be where they are.

"Every bit of me is devoted to love and art. I aspire to try to be a teacher to my young fans who feel just like I felt when I was younger. I just felt like a freak. I guess what I'm trying to say is I'm trying to liberate them, I want to free them of their fears and make them feel that they can make their own space in the world."

Lady Gaga

Saluting

Mokha Montrese

❀ ❀ ❀ *with limited editing* ❀ ❀ ❀

I was nothing but a green little gay in Louisville going to the Connection in Louisville. I was mesmerized and a little scared at what I saw. The raw emotion and talent I saw from Mokha Montrese those first nights made me want to know her.

Lucky for me it took no trying of my own. She randomly pulled me aside one night and started talking to me. A month later, I got a call asking if I wanted to drive to Chicago with her for her Miss Continental Talent rehearsal. Little did I know that that trip with this stranger would begin the fuel and love I have for DRAG pageantry and the art of female Impersonation.

This was first of many continental trips to Chicago for many bookings. I was right at home at The Connection where she coined my nickname no one had ever called me before when she needed a hand, "Mattyy." I can still hear her voice ringing in my ear even though distance has put us apart these days.

My love for Mokha is much like that for my own mother. Mokha is a source of wisdom about life and pageantry. She is always a good person to share a laugh and ultimately has been a shoulder to cry on when I needed her.

I remember that first New Year's I spent at the club away from my family and just a few years removed from my sister passing. Mokha was there to hug me and let me cry on her shoulder. Her love transcends. No matter how many times I've disappointed her, she loved me like her own child and I loved her back. I was so excited to see her achieve her long time goal of winning Miss Continental. Mokha Montrese, or as I call her Michelle, is one of my biggest role models in life.

Matthew "Mattyy" Wolfe

Saluting

Bob Taylor

❀❀❀ *with limited editing* ❀❀❀

Dear Bob,

The first time we met was in 2005 at National Entertainer of the Year. You were sitting beside me on a bench and we started talking. Little did I know at the time who you were, how big you were in our community, and how much impact you would make on my life. There are not enough words to describe how I feel about you or how much you have helped me.

I lost my real parents and had no mentor in my life. You came in and filled that role. Through your advice and guidance, I became the person and entertainer I am today. There will never be another person in my life nor in this world like you.

You are my DRAG father and it feels more like my real father. There seem to be so many things we have in common from the things we have been through in life to the fact that your name, Bob Taylor, is my father's name.

I believe everything happens for a reason. You were put on this earth to lead, teach, and help people. I am blessed to have you in my life. I love you so much.

Forever your child,

Trinity Taylor

❀ Original DRAG Handbook ❀

These messages were shared in the questionnaire posted to create the book's vibe, content, and character. Pardon the English. Many confessed later that they filled out the forms after returning from the bars.

Demonica da Bomb

Absolutely I have had help along the way. Many other queens and bar promoters stepped in to help when needed or requested. I cannot imagine anyone made it only on their own.

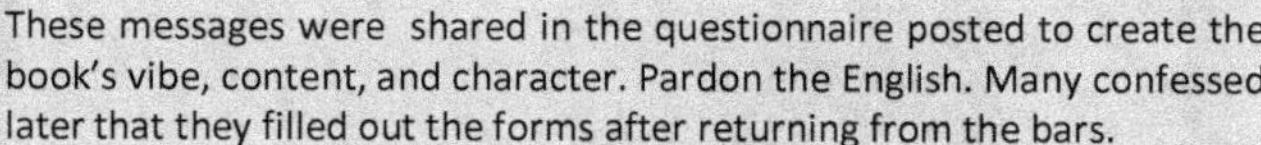

❀ Original DRAG Handbook ❀

These messages were shared in the questionnaire posted to create the book's vibe, content, and character. Pardon the English. Many confessed later that they filled out the forms after returning from the bars.

Coco Montrese

No man is an island. It takes a village create a great queen , however , some people take great pride in crediting themselves because when it comes down to it. They are the ones who have to deliver onstage and in public, many actors make great movies and win awards but someone had to write the script and hold the lights and build the set and pic the wardrobe so there's many ways to look at that. Cause still to pull it off they must be a great actor!

Eunyce Raye

I have so many people to thank.. Rudy Coggins, Brigner Milne, Rodessa Roadhard, Winnie Baygo Clair, Lil Greg, Minnie Mart, Mary K Mart are just a few...

Glitz Glam

Every entertainer I have ever met has helped me become the entertainer I am today. From lip sync techniques and make-up tips, from dance moves to character inspiration. There is no Drag University to go learn in. We all learn from each other and just tweak it our own way. Thank-you; to all the divas in my life.

Saluting

**Empress Vizcaya_Lord
and Reality Ebony Vizcaya**

❀❀❀ *with limited editing* ❀❀❀

I would love to take this time to thank my mother Empress Vizcaya Lord. She has seriously been by my side since the first day I became her daughter with an open and loving heart that she shares with everyone. Now that we are stay-away, I don't see her as often and I just want her to know that she has helped prepare me to be the performer I am today.

To my father Reality Ebony Vizcaya, I have nothing but love on top of love for you. Our mini vacations made us close. Your guidance and helping me with my makeup allowed me to grow. The both of you were there for me when I was at my lowest and with your trust and support, I am happy to carry on the family name.

Domunique Jazmin Vizcaya

"Only one person in a million becomes enlightened without a teacher's help."

Bodhidharma

Saluting

Lola Lush

❀❀❀ *with limited editing* ❀❀❀

I want to thank Lola Lush from Miami, Florida who in my early years showed me so much, and gave me tough love when needed. I am from the old school of DRAG, from the days of some of the greats (like Esme Russell who I admire). She taught me so much on how to be "a class act." I am grateful that I learned early. To be a great performer you must have great hair, makeup, nails, and wardrobe. Dana Manchester and Nikki Adams taught me the importance to connect with your audience and arrive early to meet and greet my audience.

Brittany Moore

"A self-taught man usually has a poor teacher and a worse student."

Henny Youngman

Saluting

Bob Taylor

❀❀❀ with limited editing ❀❀❀

Sitting here thinking about my DRAG father brings up so many wonderful memories and countless more lessons learned. Mr. Bob Taylor has been a blessing in my life for many years and has seen me through many different phases of life. Whether as a friend, a father, boss, or promoter, his undying love and passion for this art form and the people involved is unmatched. I feel so blessed to be a part of such a great legacy.

The story of Bob and I goes back almost seven years, when I was still discovering that cover girl doesn't cover boys. I was working at a nightclub on Merritt Island, Florida called The Rainbow Room. It was my first paying DRAG job. Bob came to see my show one night after being told about me from a good friend.

I was young and new to the industry. Little did I know, this person that I had little knowledge of, would help shape my life both professionally and personally. We spoke on and off for a while discussing DRAG and the world of pageantry. I had learned a few things before him, but never to the extent to the knowledge shared by Bob.

In 2007, I entered my first pageant with his assistance. It was Miss Brevard County. From that moment on, I went from being Shelita Cox to Shelita Taylor. Later that same year, Bob asked me to help him out with a pageant he was hosting, a big triple crowning event for Florida USofA.

I had some experience with backstage management but this was a completely new ball game. The dream team was born that night and the knowledge I gained would help me in future ventures.

We continued to produce many national award-winning pageants, focusing on success, professionalism, and sharing the love for the art of Female Impersonation.

Through these experiences, I worked with the best in the industry. I think most importantly I learned about what it means to have a "DRAG family." Bob has shown all of his kids the importance of family, and that no matter what, we will be there for each other.

With all these great experiences under my belt, I decided I wanted to try a national pageant and I knew I wanted Bob Taylor as my Promoter. Bob and I then went on an adventure I will never forget. He taught me the ins and outs of the USofA system He never lost faith in me, not to this day. I have always had his love and support, along with the rest of the Taylor Family.

I recap all these great moments and memories. I became more and more thankful for the world Bob Taylor introduced to me. He taught me through faith to trust in myself (and never take myself too seriously). With trust, I can achieve anything

Thank you, Papa Bob. I have no idea where my life or career would be if it were not for you and your continued support and love. Every day I strive to send as much love and joy into the world as you do. I hope to continue to make you proud in all that I do. Here's to many more wonderful years!

Shelita Taylor

 Original DRAG Handbook 

These messages were shared in the questionnaire posted to create the book's vibe, content, and character. Pardon the English. Many confessed later that they filled out the forms after returning from the bars.

Esme Russell

I was born into a world that did not understand what I was or why I wanted to be female when I had been born male. The gay community welcomed me, loved me , gave me work so I could support myself and placed me on stages and worshipped me . I owe the gay and lesbian community so much for their support and love. Without them, there would be no Esme. I am humbled that anyone would love me so much they would pay me, so I could do what I love so much; entertain. All I can say is thank you for the love. It makes me sad when queens show no humility and believe they deserve what they have. Everything I have ever achieved I have done it threw my hard work, but I had help club owners and patrons alike financing my life. For that I am humbled.

Saluting

**Christiana Sinclair
and Sondra Todd**

❀❀❀ *with limited editing* ❀❀❀

I have two mothers. The first, Christiana Sinclair, taught me to be the entertainer I am today, to carry myself with class, dignity, and most of all to be real, inside and out!

My second mother, Sondra Todd (also not actually my mom) treated me as if I was one of her own from the beginning. She gave me confidence when no one thought I was worth the time. Sondra taught me to be proud of myself, and the accomplishments I achieved. She showed me the way to be comfortable in my own skin as a plus size entertainer. These two mothers gave me strength through tough love, to be humble and appreciate the blessings given to me. Most of all they showed me the way to carry myself with pride, confidence, and to not let anyone make me feel less than something that I am not.

Adriana Manchez

Unedited excerpts from the files of the number one selling book on this craft,

❀ Original DRAG Handbook ❀

These messages were shared in the questionnaire.

Amy DeMilo

I've been blessed to have many great inspirations and lots of help in my career. I've been in the business so long that thanking all of them would fill this book. I thank God, my family, friends, and all those performers before me, who broke barriers, and paved the way for my future!

"If I am walking with two other men, each of them will serve as my teacher. I will pick out the good points of the one and imitate them, and the bad points of the other and correct them in myself."

Confucius

Saluting

Cassi Welch

❀❀❀ *with limited editing* ❀❀❀

Cassi Welch was a gorgeous, curvaceous, blond, dancing queen who excelled in her craft and loves DRAG so much that she wanted to help others do well too. My DRAG mother approached me well into my career after seeing that I was trying to get better, but wasn't doing things exactly right. She asked me if I would allow her to paint me one night. Of course, I said yes.

From that point on, she began to show me what to wear, how to wear it, and helped me to be a better DRAG queen. She gave me her last name, achieved paid bookings for me to gain stage experience, and watched my career find its true path.

To this day, she continues to help in any way she can. We spend holidays together; hang out on a regular basis, just as I do my biological mother. Without Cassi's influence, I would not be the entertainer that I am today. I know plenty of DRAG mothers who tag someone with a name, show them a thing or two and fall out of the picture.

Cassi's from a different school. She guides where needed, develops every aspect of a queen. She demands excellence, dignity, pride, respect, and just a hint of Diva. She gives the same in return. I thank God that Cassi helped me become who I am.

MiMi Welch

"The dream begins with a teacher who believes in you, who tugs and pushes and leads you to the next plateau, sometimes poking you with a sharp stick called "truth."

Dan Rather

Saluting

Bob Taylor and
James Brown

❀❀❀ with limited editing ❀❀❀

The first fourteen or so years of my career, I was "in a word," the entertainer named China. I took the last name "Noones" because I learned from so many people about the art of female impersonation and the lifestyle that comes with it. I learned from Tiffany Wellington, Sondra Todd, Tina Knight, and James Brown (RIP) just to name a few. I spent my early years denying my need to belong to something more substantial, some identity beyond the character or characters that I created for stage and for the public. I have been very successful in my career but not in the art of trust.

Eventually I gained wisdom through time and experience combined with many pitfalls. I curved my need for independence and found myself wanting not only advice, but also the nurturing that comes along with having a "DRAG father/mother," and family.

I have an amazing biological mother. The love and care I have received over the last six years since I staked a claim to the Taylor name has been a blessing. I could easily joined the "House of Todd." I am proud of my name and gay family, and to Bob Taylor.

I thank you Bob for picking me from the darkness where James left off. I am humbled and I love you.

To Sondra Todd, you have seen it all my love. I have known you since I snuck in to gay bars as a minor. Thank you for never giving up on me. I am grateful for your honesty, compassion, and most of all your respect. I guess it is all really just the law of attraction at work.

James Brown, the former owner of Metro in Jacksonville, Florida mentored me. He was born December 31st and passed away on July 4, 2006 (talk about arriving and leaving with a bang). He was my original DRAG daddy and truly a father to me. He taught me both the business and promotional side to female impersonation. He showed me how to talk to people, how to be strong and courageous even if it meant standing alone or being alone. Many of our "battles of will" ended with me realizing he was right. James did a lot for the gay, lesbian and transgendered (especially transgendered) community, not only in Jacksonville, but abroad.

His support took a dear friend, Alexandria Gabrielle Sherrington on to win the Miss Gay USA pageant in Dallas, Texas. He did things like this for so many girls though. Though I was the first and was always proud of this, I learned through him to respect others and myself. I only wish he were still here to see the real outcome of so many things and to say, I love you once more...

China Taylor

Saluting

Teriko St. James

❀❀❀ with limited editing ❀❀❀

Let me write about my relationship with my father Teriko Perkins, aka Teriko St. James. It is actually funny how we met. I had just won a pageant in Columbus, Georgia. After the show, I went to Waffle House to grab a bite to eat with my friends. Upon arrival, I noticed Kortni Bone't, my father back then, so I joined his table. Teriko was with him (they were lovers).

We instantly clicked after introducing ourselves. We did not speak for a while after that evening, but I thought about him all the time! One day I was at home and a cellphone text message came in from Teriko. I was overjoyed. He called me from his job at the hotel and we talked for hours!

Most gay parents only have kids to have to add them to their collection of names, but it is so different with my daddy and me. We have a bond that is so unstoppable and so indescribable that it is often eerie.

We share a similar fashion sense, we like the same foods, drinks, and we love to party. It is actually, like we are really family. We support each other in our pageantry careers; we give each other valuable, constructive criticism that indeed helps both of us progress in our fields.

Not only do we motivate each other in the gay world, but we push each other in reality. I'm a college student and he always checks my grades, along with my extracurricular activities.

My father is everything to me. I love him so much. The men in my life that I considered father figures have passed. I really hold the relationship. He's an amazing man. Teriko is funny, kind, giving, honest, with a heart of pure country, Alabama gold! We both plan to compete at Mr. Black Universe in the fall. I am going to fight for the title, but support my father. One of us will be victorious.

A true friendship and child-parent relationship shares no jealously, no backbiting, no lies, just pure love!
No one will ever be able to take his place in my life or my heart.

Armondis Bone't

Unedited excerpts from the files of the
Number one selling book on this craft,

❀ Original DRAG Handbook ❀

These messages were shared in the questionnaire posted to create the book's vibe, content, and character. Pardon the English. Many confessed later that they filled out the forms after returning from the bars.

Jocelyn Summers

I have taken a little bit of every entertainer I have ever watched and have been advised by. Weather good or bad I took the info and decided on your own path.. as the saying goes.. "It takes a village..."

Maxine Padlock

Everyone has someone to thank. People forget even the ones that put us down have to be thanked cause it may be them that makes us stride to be better. I have to thank my Estranged Drag Mother Phoebe Darnell (Erik) and my Adoptive Drag Mother Kathryn Conover. Gurls that helped in makeup like Desiree Dubois and Misty Eyez. Sometimes it helps to know why you do something rather than how to do it. I thank Carlos and Stanley previous owners of the infamous Trixie's (RIP) for giving Drag Queens a place to start. I thank Justice Royal for letting me do my 1st performance on Trixie's stage. Mike let me perform the backstage of the Copa. And all my sisters I learned so much from watching you all at Trixie's and Copa and Bills Filling Station. I love all of you!

Saluting

Daneé Russo

❀❀❀ *with limited editing* ❀❀❀

DRAG mother Daneé Russo, may she rest in peace, taught me how to be a true lady. Thanks to her, the streets of Chicago did not eat me alive; she took me under her wing at the young age of seventeen.

Daneé groomed me to be a national entertainer. I became her number one project, as she groomed me to become her successor in the entertainment world.

She moved me with her to Pennsylvania, helped my career to succeed, eventually allowing me to own the Miss Pennsylvania USofA.

I learned from her how to be a good person. She inspired me to help those afflicted with HIV in our community. If she were still alive, she would be very proud of me. I will never forget her.

Thank you Miss Daneé Russo. I could not have had a better DRAG mother; I will love you forever.

Your daughter,

Monique Trudeau

"A teacher is a person who never says anything once."

Howard Nemerov

Saluting

Mavis Codfish

❀❀❀ *with limited editing* ❀❀❀

My DRAG mom is the funniest bitch I know. Mrs. Mavis Codfish is a cast member at Lion's Den in Lake City, Florida. My DRAG career started on October 31, 2011. We held our first amateur night. I performed to the song, "I Will Always Love You" by Whitney Houston. I remember my DRAG mom came to me at the end of the song to hug me. She told me I did a good job, which made me feel like a million bucks. My DRAG mom always helps me with wigs, outfits, and makeup. She is awesome.

Simeon Codfish

Unedited excerpts from the files of the
Number one selling book on this craft,

❈ Original DRAG Handbook ❈

These messages were shared in the questionnaire posted to create the book's vibe, content, and character. Pardon the English. Many confessed later that they filled out the forms after returning from the bars.

Ororo Summers
Either for or against you, if you take the energy they are sending to you it can make you a stronger person. Drag is hard and you have to be mentally tough to be able to stand it.

Lady Tajma Hall
Success is what you make it! In life, you will have supporters and haters. It is up to you to decide whom you will follow. No one can do anything to you that you do not allow!

Joey Brooks
I owe it all to my Drag mother Brenda Dee. In addition, I thank Tommy Jackson and Tony Wadell.

> **"I'm embarrassed every time
> I look a teacher in the eye,
> because we ask them
> to do so much for so little."**
>
> Phil McGraw

Saluting

Karrissa Wade
and Wolfie

❀❀❀ with limited editing ❀❀❀

I live in Orange Park, Florida. In 2007, I moved here from Brooklyn, New York. I have been performing since about 2005 but the twist is, when I started out performing, I started out as a "Kitten." A kitten is a biological female who performs like a DRAG performer, but not in DRAG; just a typical Girly Foo Foo.

My DRAG mama is the mouth of the South, Miss Karrissa Wade." I have to tell you, her name says it all. My DRAG Daddy is the male illusionist "Wolfie." From the very beginning, I was a spoiled baby! I was daddy's little girl, and Mama's princess. Looking back it is hysterical.

I started out as their daughter! I learned so very much from both my DRAG parents and to say that I adore them would be a huge understatement. From Mama, I learned humor, stage presence, and the ability to interact with the audience. I have always admired her ability to make people laugh under any circumstances.

From my "Pops," lessons came later. I was a female performer, with a father that was quick to right me when I was wrong, give me advice, and lend a helping hand. When I became a male illusionist, he offered me his time, patience, and knowledge. I used to watch him and another mentor Gage Gatlyn transform. It amazed me.

In about 2007, I went from being their daughter, to becoming their son.

Like most children, I needed guidance from all ends, not just in the performing world. Both my DRAG parents gave me unconditional love, even when I was messing up and acting the fool. Too often I have seen DRAG parents give up on their kids when they would screw up, not mine. There is not a day that goes by that I am not grateful.

They both took me under wings to give me structure, passion, and respect for the art craft of DRAG. They filled my brain with as much knowledge as I could soak up. I knew no matter what, I could count on them both in and out of the DRAG world.

I got sick once. I asked my daddy to make me chicken soup to make it feel better, he did. I got upset one night at some crazy hour, called my mama. She listened with not only her ears but her heart as well without once complaining.

With them, it is truly about "family" first, DRAG second. They both put me in my place when I need it; give me unconditional love, and support. They taught me much over the years about performing and perfecting my craft. More importantly, they taught me when you take on a DRAG child it's like adopting a child, it's for life.

They set amazing examples both on and off the stage, which I pay forward with my own DRAG son. In my opinion, I have the BEST DRAG parents ever!

AJ Menendez

Saluting

Magenta Dupree

❀❀❀ *with limited editing* ❀❀❀

At the age of eighteen, I stepped into the world of DRAG. Under the hot stage lights, I felt nervous having all these eyes on me while I was dressed in DRAG for the very first time. Now at the age of twenty-one, I've come a long way. I've preformed several times and have made some memories that will last a lifetime. Along the way, I picked up an amazing DRAG mother. Magenta Dupree has been one of the best DRAG mothers I could ask for. Although we live in different states, she is always giving me advice and trying to help me any way possible. When tears are in my eyes at 3 am, she is always a phone call away. I'm looking forward to many performances with her and the opportunity to use the things she has to teach me about DRAG.

Diamond Dupree

"If you have knowledge, let others light their candles at it."

Margaret Fuller

❀ Original DRAG Handbook ❀

These messages were shared in the questionnaire posted to create the book's vibe, content, and character. Pardon the English. Many confessed later that they filled out the forms after returning from the bars.

Tabatha Lovall

Many people helped me succeed. Many of them Fans. But mostly other entertainers who took the time to encourage me to keep on.

Ginger Minj

I believe in the power of family and community. Without them, I would look frightful, and probably be performing for the crickets and the brick walls!

Saluting

Tyria Inman

❀❀❀ *with limited editing* ❀❀❀

Dear Tyria Iman,

I want to start out by saying you have been the best DRAG mother. I remember when I was getting ready to compete for my first pageant. I was not yet an Iman. You came to Virginia to help dress me.

Do you also remember when I performed the wedding scene at a national pageant? You fell out on the floor rolling around. You played my mother in the talent that was a kiki. The talent was sickening. You always make it a family thing. You bring along my siblings and many other family members to support my performances in Washington D.C. and New York just to name a few.

You taught me to learn things on my own, taking time to invest in my craft as an entertainer. I remember the times I did not listen. I gagged in the end. Most children don't listen to their parents. I always looked up to you as one of the best role models. It goes farther than just being my gay mother.

We have a great friendship. The friendship we cherished before you became my gay mother. In the mid-nineties, I was a go-go dancer. I had no experience in make-up.

I remember when you said, "Come over here, you can't go out there on that stage looking like Casper."

You painted my face before I hit the stage. The little things matter to me the most. Those little things make such a big difference in your role as my gay mother. I take one-step, you took two steps to help me succeed. I am so grateful to have you as my gay mother and as my friend. I don't get a chance to see you as much. I miss being in your presence. Your support is the best. Words cannot explain how much you are there for me. I dedicate this letter to you with love. If you were sitting right next to me, I would read this letter to you. I would have greeted you with a big hug after reading this letter to you. I love you always.

Your Son,

Stefon Royce Iman

Saluting

**Starina Stjames
And Joey D.**

❀❀❀ with limited editing ❀❀❀

Dear Starina, my mama,

Look how time flies.

You were there when I took my very first step on stage two years ago. I was fresh to the DRAG world and didn't know where to go. You sat there and watched me grow to turn into the king I am today. They say home is where the heart is. My heart lies with the Stjames.

Just because we are not blood does not mean we are not family. You treat me as your son. When I am not sure, you give me a kick in the butt to get up to give a hundred and ten percent. You always remind us that we do not put on a show for a dollar in our pocket, but for the smile we leave when we walk off stage.

You have taught me never doubt myself, to hold my head high, and be proud to be "Jayden." You are my guiding star in the dimmest of nights and only a phone call away. You are beautiful. I love you from the bottom of my heart. Thanks for being you mama!

Love always your baby boy,
Jayden Stjames

____

Dear Joey, my father,

Wow, how do I begin?

Joey you are an absolutely amazing inspiration to me. I consider you my DRAG father. You were the reason I became a DRAG king. I saw you the very first time at Hamburger Mary's.

I felt a chill in my heart and running through my veins. I knew after that show, the path I sought for myself. I wanted to make an audience smile. I wanted to feel the rush.

You showed me I could go out there to be myself. As long as I dreamed it, I could be it. You have always been the kindest, sweetest friendliest king I know. You always give me advice when I need it the most and I thank you for always being there and supporting me. I strive to improve myself more and more to one day be able to shine beside you in your light. Joey, you are an amazing person inside and out and people are so lucky to know you and have you in their lives and I am thankful to be one of those people. Thank you for your words of encouragement and guidance. Love always

Jayden Stjames

Saluting

**Shirleena and
Miss Reena Rossie**

❀❀❀ *with limited editing* ❀❀❀

I had help from day one from wonderful people who took an interest in an underage kid. I had people watching out for me with big hearts and kinc souls. Maybe the era I started in made the difference in my life. It is not always easy, but life is an incredible journey!

Shirleena, who I met at the Ice Palace on Fire Island, took a big interest in me; she showed me the importance of the art of the lip-syncing.

She drummed into my head "They only look at the outfit for 30 seconds, after that you better have the talent to back it up. Baby you are out there to entertain them, besides if you make a mistake they really don't know what your choreography is, but if you aren't on spot with your lip sync, it's over!"

When I first started, like most of the girls, my makeup was not as hot as I thought it was. Shileena was fast to point it out, as we sat in the dressing room of the Ice Palace on Fire Island. She said, "Baby you know I love you, but you really need to learn how to paint your face. That fish makeup just doesn't work; we have beards to cover up."

She used to call it "hormone troubles." She said I used the wrong type of base makeup, than taught me about 'Stein's Velvet Stick' which covered everything and gave me a flawless finish. I may be dating myself, since they do not make Stein's Velvet Stick anymore. Now I use 'Dermablend'.

My friend Bobby from Long Island, who was a Barbara Streisand impersonator, was the one who really taught me how to paint like a Diva. Bobby said, "Never go on stage without a complete set of upper and lower lashes."

She showed me how to paint my eyes like a Las Vegas Show Girl. The point is to pass as a real girl, just better, bigger and with flair. Bobby got a hold of me one day and he entered me in a contest at the 'Silver Lining' in Queens, New York. He let me use an outfit of his and I was still learning the words to "Cher's Dark Lady" in my old Fiat X 1/9 on the way to the club.

I was a wreck and did not want to go through with it. Bobby gave me all the encouragement in the world but still left me no way out. To this day, I will never forget that night. I won my first contest as "Miss Silver Lining." There was another special soul in my life, "Miss Reena Rossie," a NY girl so sweet and equally talented. I had such a crush on him as a boy, but he never knew it. Back then, DRAG mothers never crossed that line, they always watched out for us younger girls. Reena was the first to get me to travel to perform. She went to my mom and paved the way for my first big road trip with the girls, when I was just a teenager.

It was to a little bar in upstate New York in Lake George. I can remember it like it was yesterday. The kitchen of the old house I grew up in on Long Island, with that god awful floral wall paper looked like someone smashed tomatoes on black patent leather. My mom was grilling Reena with her usual twenty questions. She stood there with her arms crossed while Reena let her know she would watch out for me. She told my mom not to worry; as she would make sure I was safe and nothing would happen to me.

I couldn't get a word in edge wise, so I just sat there watching. I could hear what Reena was saying, but mom sounded like the schoolteacher in the Charlie Brown cartoon,

"Wa wa wa."

After what seemed like a never-ending session of embracement for me, Reena got mom to give in and say yes. Writing about these memories now brings me right back to those days. Funny the things that forever stay with you as you go through life. This is the love of a DRAG Mother along with a Mothers Love. "See you in the Dungeon."

Mis Sadistic

**"Tell me and I forget.
Teach me and I remember.
Involve me and I learn."**

Benjamin Franklin

Unedited excerpts from the files of the
Number one selling book on this craft,

❀ Original DRAG Handbook ❀

These messages were shared in the questionnaire posted to create the book's vibe, content, and character. Pardon the English. Many confessed later that they filled out the forms after returning from the bars.

Patrice Knight

I can thank many great performers. Kim Ross, Bobby Lake, Esme Russell, Tiffany Middlesexx, Joey Brooks, Appolonia, and Taryn Michaels. Eachtook me under their wings. I thank The New Connection Night Club in St. Pete (now Georgie's Alibi) for giving me my first Show Host job.

Twat Sisters

We believe all our friends and fans in the gay/straight/bi community has made us who we are today. Some of the people that have helped us along the way include our Drag Mother Holly Girl, Miss Joey Brooks, Tiffani Middlesexx, Dana Manchester, Tiffany Ariagus, Melanie Minyon, and most importantly our moms.

Unedited excerpts from the files of the
Number one selling book on this craft,

❀ Original DRAG Handbook ❀

These messages were shared in the questionnaire posted to create the book's vibe, content, and character. Pardon the English. Many confessed later that they filled out the forms after returning from the bars.

Danika Fierecë

There's one girl who has helped me more than anyone ever could in this industry. She's rode me pretty hard and I appreciate every minute of it. I can honestly say I am what I am as a performer because of her and her contest.

ShaeShae LaReese

Everyone helps you.

LaKeisha Pryce

I'm had a lot of people in my career that have always been behind me whether it was other performers, friends, family, etc. and I'm very grateful to have them now or have had them at all in my corner.

Monique Michaels

I have had some amazing people behind me in every endeavor as an entertainer. I thank my parents, jobs, friends, other entertainers. I have been amazingly blessed to have the love and support I needed to grow and fly as a female illusionist.

Raven Manniac

When I was starting out, there was ONE person who took me under his wing and made sure that I was headed in the right direction.

Stephen Brooks

Learn from the best, and ya learn from the WORST! But, most of us are surrounded by our sisters, that to pick out one or two is tough!!

Saluting

Desiree Mathews,
Jodie Santana, and
Clarissa Cavalier

❀❀❀ *with limited editing* ❀❀❀

When I initially looked at the expectations of this latest DRAG project, I was like, cool beans I can do this.However, as I began to write my letter, it became truly difficult for me to keep moving forward and remain focused. I came to the realization that I had been a big ol' hand full when I was a baby queen. I had a host of mothers, though I am sure a few will not claim me today! Each one taught me something very different and truly made a dynamic impact on the entertainer and adult I became in life.

My introduction to the art of illusion was via the larger than life Desiree Mathews. Sure, she is a few months younger than I am, but she set the bar high for me when I announced that I wanted to learn how to paint. Off to Walgreen's and Merle Norman for a few supplies for her to teach me with, the mall for some clothes and a bra, pan stick, powder, stuff for the lips and eyes, duct tape, panty hose, and the list went on and on.

Geez, over two-hundred dollars spent by the time they bagged my collection. Mind you, it was 1987 when a dang Hardee's check sure didn't go far! We sat at the kitchen table to spackle my face. Ironically, when we were done with the first paint job, I looked like I was primed and spackled for real. We laughed and took photos. Thankfully, most of those photos have been lost over the past twenty-five years or so. Naturally, things did improve with practice, new makeup, and more money to invest.

With the basic skills in place, I began placing my tush up the stages around southeast Iowa and western Illinois. I learned quickly that all the big smiles and laughter that took place on the stage did not always carry back into the dressing rooms.

My second mother was Jodie Santana. When I began doing DRAG, Jodie had already arrived. She was a superstar of sorts to me. The audience came to their feet when she took stage. She was the kind of entertainer I wanted to become when I "grew up." I would lurk around in the dressing room at JR's hoping to have a conversation with Jodie. Most of the time she didn't have time to talk, as she was a working woman. Dang it!

Finally, one evening after an "open stage night," her ride was late. I finally had the chance to talk to her. I wanted to know how to be as good as her. I just knew there was a secret to it. Do you know what she told me?

She said, "Practice and always doing what makes you comfortable."

Well, duh, I knew that. I wanted her secret dang it, but that was Jodie's secret. I've known her, for a couple of decades now, she's always been the epitome of someone comfortable in their own skin. This was the secret to her success. The most important mother to me, was the person who pulled me aside one night when I was being a little shady after an open stage event to "chat" with me

She said, "Desiree's brother. Come here, I need to talk now. I heard what you just said to that boy. It was wrong; really wrong Jay."

I told the young man he could take his Goodwill clothes and shoes out to the alley and do some hooking to make quick money instead of begging guys in the bar for a dollar, because he was taking my tips! I didn't realize the boy, at perhaps seventeen years old was looking for money to help take care of his homeless mother, unable to work, because of HIV. She lost her job because her job discovered she was positive in the late nineties. His mother lost her insurance along with her job; and couldn't qualify for any kind of assistance because her good paying job with John Deere complicated matters for applying to programs based on previous year income levels.

Now she was unemployed and homeless. He just needed a few dollars to help his mother. I felt like such an ass. I gave the kid the money that I had made that night and drove him to the place they now were forced to call home. Each time I crossed his path I would give him money and a ride. To this day, I hang out with him and now his wife. Clarissa Cavalier was an absolutely amazing entertainer, a true role model for me, with stellar talent, and was taken far too soon from us. More than that though, she gave all she had to anyone that was truly in need. Clarissa taught me more about the realities of life and judgment in that one conversation than anyone in my life had before or after that few minutes in the corner of a bar.

Over the years, I have been blessed with an amazing family. I have learned many things to share from so many incredible entertainers. Desiree, Jodie, and Clarissa, thank you for each and everything that you shared with me. You shaped me into the person I am today, both in and out of DRAG!

Most of all, thank you for teaching me that the family we choose is as strong, if not stronger, than the family we are born into as children. I love the three of you more that you will ever realize.

Demonica da Bomb

Saluting

Buttwiser

❀❀❀ *with limited editing* ❀❀❀

I remember the first time he set foot in my bar. I was barely twenty-one, wet behind the ears and loving every second of attention showered on me by a bunch of gorgeous queens. I had heard of the "famous" Buttwiser and was thoroughly unimpressed with his appearance and was irritated he was in my bar.

He had the nerve to ask me to come to his bar to watch a show. I spoke with my friend Spencer, who introduced me to DRAG. Spencer said I should check it out since Buttwiser was a well-known king. My friend noted, I should feel honored to have been personally asked by the entertainer. I went and saw his show. I was unimpressed and quickly went back to living my life.

Flash forward a half dozen years.

I had been in and out of performing, including an overseas deployment. The bar I began performing in changed and ultimately stopped having shows. I found myself adrift. I happened on a MySpace message from the entertainer Logan Rider, asking me if I would like to come to the Buttwiser Bash show. Logan asked if I would be interested in performing at the Bash since I listed on my MySpace page that I previously entertained as a DRAG performer.

After taking another look at the event, I called the emcee… Buttwiser. It was a match made in heaven or was that hell? I started performing regularly again with the 2007 Bash and haven't really been out of DRAG for longer than six months since then. He gave me a home.

Buttwiser is an amazing entertainer who continues to change the face of DRAG in Kansas City. His Bash show celebrated its ninth anniversary this year. We have not always gotten along. There have been bad times as well as good, but I have never known a person with more patience. Through subtle hints, kindness, critiques, and an occasional two by four upside the head, he transformed that cocky, young, arrogant performer entertainer into a seasoned, successful DRAG king and male impersonator.

I could not have asked a better person to call my DRAG dad and friend. Today I am still honored to have the privilege of still calling him both friend and father. I hope that someday he gets to open the pages of this book and read all about how much he means to me.

Thank you, Buttwiser, for all that you do!

Mr. Colin Grey

Saluting

**Mokha Montrese
and Bob Taylor**

❀❀❀ *with limited editing* ❀❀❀

A family is not of mere flesh and blood, but of the heart and soul. It creates parents and creates children. I perform in DRAG for fun, charitable functions, and not as a career. I have had so many people in the gay entertainment community helped to forge my love for DRAG, female and male impersonation, and other LGBT shows.

I consider my true and first DRAG mother, Mokha Montrese, whom I met in 1996. She is not the first female impersonator I ever saw, but she is the first professional to create with me a true friendship. Our immediate connection grew through the years and continues today. I helped her for a while with shows and almost every pageant she entered for the first few years. I still, to this day, tell performers her secret for cleaning and styling synthetic hair wigs.

My job I got because of her at the World Famous Parliament House as a lighting technician. She helped me meet so many important people that are still of the best friends. She taught me so much in the beginning and I will love her and her awesome talent forever. I am the first born DRAG son of Bob Taylor, a.k.a. "The Living Legend," Legend Infinti, Poppa Bear, Pops, and many other names that may or may not be flattering or printable. I met him through Mokha.

My introduction to him was in 1996 at the Parliament House. We "sat at opposite ends of the table," so to speak. Almost a year passed before things started to change for us. One night in the dressing room, prior to me becoming an employee, I stood my ground and it changed both how things were done at the resort and my friendships with many of the performers including Tiffany McCray, Darcel Stevens, Sierrah Foxx, and Miss P.

Soon after, Scott Cammack hired me. He was Bob Taylor's husband. Our friendships blossomed and grew over the past sixteen years. We have been through so much in our time together. I could not even begin to list everything. Trust me it includes drama, craziness, happiness, fun times, sad moments, fights and make-ups.

Bob Taylor is one of the best, if not the best, pageant promoters in the industry. He made me his right-hand man (and sometimes left) in almost every pageant he produced. We became a well-oiled pageant machine.

I have seen our family grow and grow. He accepts anyone and everyone as they are and helps them to find the person they want to be. He has done more for people than anyone will ever know. He shares with many, but only opens up completely with a lucky few. I consider myself one of the lucky people. I jokingly say to him that he has to stop "spreading his seed" around so much.

For Bob, seed is defined by his loving, caring, and uplifting ways. He listens, loves, and guides people in the direction of their choice, while offering them alternate options they may not have considered. He has an infectious spirit shared freely with his children. Bob is loved by so many people, including myself. My life is forever changed.

Christopher Todd Guy

Unedited excerpts from the files of the
Number one selling book on this craft,

❀ Original DRAG Handbook ❀

These messages were shared in the questionnaire posted to create the book's vibe, content, and character. Pardon the English. Many confessed later that they filled out the forms after returning from the bars.

Champagne T. Bordeaux

Never forget where you come from, make sure those whom have been there for you know you feel nothing but love for them. I hope I can give back a fraction of what I have received from them.

Deva DaVyne

My blood mother for always standing by me, my beautiful group of friends, my flawless drag mother, and drag children for constantly teaching me that I'm loved and it helps keep me driven each time I go out and see the smiles on the club patrons faces.

Melissa Morgan

First I owe our lord, parents, and family for being here for me, with much love and support. Many friends including Ricky, Manny, Aaron Carl Tori Holden, Sybil Storm the Late Great Tasha Diane and the late great, Jessica Jackson, Ric, and My family gets bigger every day and they all mean the world to me.

Miss Gigi

I owe everyone who has helped me in my drag more than I could ever repay them. I continue

Saluting

Mr. Chance Wise

❀❀❀ with limited editing ❀❀❀

Chance started out as my friend before I came out as Teresa LeCroix. We would laugh and play around about different things. It was not until September 25th that I had asked him to be my DRAG father; he hesitantly accepted.

It was strange on the inside to be a DRAG queen with a DRAG father since they are total opposites like straight couples. However, we stuck it out. I helped him with his make-up and he helped me create my appearance. Unlike most guys, he spoke what he truly thought. I took his critiques to heart and improved myself with the help of some other DRAG queens who have also grown to be a part of my family.

Chance always had a hard time helping me improve since he clearly does not dress up like a woman. He gave me ideas for each performance. He explained my flaws while rooting for me, so I can make them my strengths. As a performer, we always need to have our support crew in the audience and he is my crew chief. Even when we may not be on the same page (and argue to the point of killing each other), we still support each other.

We were at McDonalds one night, after almost hitting an ambulance, and I paid for his meal. While we stood by our cars preparing to leave, we started a conversation concerning trans men. He spoke about a certain DRAG king who takes "T" to lower his voice and literally be more like a man.

"So if I stop drinking tea, my voice will be higher pitched and more feminine?" I asked from under my blond wig.

He looked at me for a few seconds before bursting into laughter. Funny part is that I was being serious until he explained to me "T" is a hormone, not the drink.

We still laugh to this day about my 'Blonde' moment.

Teresa LeCroix-Wise

Uneditec excerpts from the files of the
Number one selling book on this craft,

❀ Original DRAG Handbook ❀

These messages were shared in the questionnaire posted to create the book's vibe, content, and character. Pardon the English. Many confessed later that they filled out the forms after returning from the bars.

Amanda Love

I owe everyone, but most of all God; without him I would not be here. My ex for pushing me to succeed, and all of my drag family without you Amanda would not have succeeded.

Ada Buffet

I have been inspired by many, helped without strings by few. I thank LuLu LaDiva, Lucy Lushus, and Chantel McKee (spiritually).

Michelle Tatum

I have had many people help me out on my journey, and am grateful for those people. I always call them my Glam Squad.

Naomi D-Lish

You aren't a good performer if you aren't willing to learn. During shows that I am in, I always try to watch the other performers and take notes. I can see what 'I do and do not like. What should and shouldn't I do. EVERY drag queen I have ever seen has helped me; every one of them!

Selina Kyle

I feel that had people not given us a shot, or had shown their support in me I would not have made it this far. Thank you for your help, support, and thank you to everyone who continues to support our art.

Saluting

Jayda Clyne

❀❀❀ *with limited editing* ❀❀❀

Dear Jayda,

We have been down a long road of growth together as mother and daughter. Ever since the first time I saw you perform a few years ago I am amazed by your stage presence and how graceful you were. You supported me in the beginning before I was actually painting. I would get on stage with the dance music and try to lip-sync the words while doing some kind of odd dance move.

Later on when I was down and depressed you called me, concerned, to make sure I was going to be ok. You put the true meaning to the title DRAG mother. I remember the night Celyndra was born; we sat talking on the phone when I told you I wanted to do DRAG. You told me that if I want to be your DRAG daughter that you would be honored to have me. I was excited that you were willing to take a chance not knowing if I would be any good.

Time has passed and I have grown with your help and guidance to get me where I need to go. You stood by me when I did my first national pageant. I had never done a pageant before, since I was only performing for the past few months.

You were there for my talent shows, performances, and pageant, while balancing your own demanding full time job. I know our schedules have made it difficult lately to spend quality time together, but I look forward to the future. We still have to do those side-by-side windmills on stage.

As your daughter, I promise to be my best on stage. I promise to show the world who we are and hold the last name of Clyne with pride. I love you and I am so happy that you are my DRAG mother. I will forever let the world know I am Jayda Clyne's daughter.

Celyndra Lashay Clyne

Saluting

Jacquelyn St James

❀ ❀ ❀ *with limited editing* ❀ ❀ ❀

I want to take a minute to let everyone know that my DRAG mother is the greatest. Jacquelyn leads our families with four branches while still managing to make each of us feel special. Our family tree has girls, boys, queens, and kings, and all of us have a place in her heart. Her love does not stay in a dressing room either. She makes sure that we all know, in DRAG and in life, we are important.

Jacquelyn always love us and enables us to find our own way, while making it easy for us to come back home to her. When I am in need or hurt, she is the first person I know I can call on the phone. She is an amazing Amazon woman teaching us to love and live. From our first brush stroke of fuchsia La Femme eye shadow to the last line of a song, she guides us and lets us fly free. She loves unconditionally.

I am one of her female children, just starting my own career in DRAG. I have yearned to learn to grow with my sisters and brothers. When I was ready, she was ready with me. She may get angry with us and hurt by us, but she keeps us in her heart.

She is struggling and my heart aches to know we sometimes cannot do anything but be there for her. I hope she knows just how loved she is as our Matriarch. She brought me into DRAG, showed me the way, encourages my life, and proudly named me as well. Our family would not be a family without her. I love my mamma Jacquelyn St James. There is no one else in the world like her and I am glad to call her mine. With love,

Candice St. James

"I touch the future,
I teach."

Christa McAuliffe

Note: For those that forgot already, Christa McAuliffe is the teacher that perished in the Challenger Space Shuttle explosion.

Unedited excerpts from the files of the
Number one selling book on this craft,

❀ Original DRAG Handbook ❀

These messages were shared in the questionnaire posted to create the book's vibe, content, and character. Pardon the English. Many confessed later that they filled out the forms after returning from the bars.

Katrina Starr

In my short ten months of performing, I find that everyone I have met has helped me in some way or another. Those who had bad things to say or a negative attitude to me or my craft made my skin thicker and prepared me for the future because I'm sure I'll face worse people and attitudes in my years to come.

Saluting

Wendy Williams

❀❀❀ *with limited editing* ❀❀❀

My DRAG mother is Wendy Williams, I don't perform in DRAG. I am a promoter and pageant owner. Wendy Williams of Lexington, Kentucky took me in as her DRAG son and taught me how to be a promoter and to do it well. She taught me, it is not about the money, pageant, or fame, but the girls!

Wendy has always been one of the most influential people in my career and my personal life. She told me to be constantly true to myself. The most important thing she ever told me was to never stop being real,

"You may be disliked, but you will always be respected," she added!
Words I live by to this day!

Justin Barnes Williams

"By learning you will teach; by teaching you will understand."

Latin Proverb

Saluting

**Victoria Bacon
and Anson Reign**

❀❀❀ *with limited editing* ❀❀❀

I personally created Ivanna Dooche with the inspiration from Pandora DeStrange and The Arizona Gender Outlaws. One night I showed up to one of their shows in DRAG looking like a hot tranny mess. I got booked in two shows that night surprisingly enough for Anson Reign's and the other for Victoria Bacon's show, DRAGtini. I enjoyed both shows a lot and gained a lot of experience from it.

A special place is in my heart for those two performers since they helped me with my start in DRAG. I consider Anson and Bacon my adopted parents.

Victoria continues to help me, as I am now a permanent member of her show. I continuously learn from all the performers in her show. I am eternally grateful to Victoria Bacon, Felicia Minor, and Tabatha Lovall for their   support.

Ivanna Dooche

Uneditec excerpts from the files of the
Number one selling book on this craft,

❀ Original DRAG Handbook ❀

These messages were shared in the questionnaire posted to create the book's vibe, content, and character. Pardon the English. Many confessed later that they filled out the forms after returning from the bars.

Rhyana Vorhman
I should say everyone that has helped me be who I am today. I am grateful for my husband, family, friends, and coworkers.

Shugah Caine
I have many friends and loved ones who have supported me. I found that many folks would smile in your face as they stab you in the back. Not all, but we know the bitchy queens are out there.

Top Ten History's Greatest Teachers

Even the Greatest of Teachers began with one simple hope to make a difference

Annie Sullivan
(1866-1936)

By the age of four, Annie Sullivan was legally blind due to a disease called trachoma. At age nine, she was sent to an orphanage that lacked formal education opportunities. She pleaded with an administrator to be allowed to learn and eventually graduated as valedictorian of the Perkins School for the Blind in 1886. After several operations resulted in a return of her partial eyesight, she used her gifts and uncommon perspective to begin teaching a young deaf and mute girl named Helen Keller. Sullivan was the first teacher to find success with a deaf and mute child. She helped her student transition from an undisciplined seven year old to a graduate of Radcliffe College.

"Education is the mother of leadership."

Wendell L. Willkie

Saluting

Bob Taylor and
Dana Douglas

❀❀❀ with limited editing ❀❀❀

I knew things were going to be interesting when at the age of seven, you could not tell me that I wasn't Snow White. She was who I wanted to be. would put on my grandma's heels. They had a three-inch heel (so tall to me then) and they had the cutest bow right on the top of the foot. I grew up in a tiny town in Ohio.

As you can imagine I did not have much culture, so I kept my feelings secret. Around the age of eighteen, I began experimenting in dressing glamorously (if you know what I mean). I messed around with that for a while, not doing anything big with it.

My first big night was a masquerade in Huntington, West Virginia at the Stone Wall bar. I went as a fairy, I felt so beautiful with my platinum hair. My roommate helped me with my makeup.

Can you guess my name at the time?

I cringe when I think about it. Starla Jade! Friends helped me come up with Starla, because I resembled Pamela Anderson and I loved stars at the time. I had so much fun that night knowing small town country life wasn't for me. I was different, and I wanted to be myself without worrying. I wanted to see more of everything and it was not in Piketon, Ohio.

When I moved to Florida, I started trying to be a star. It was rough, and it took me a while to learn everything. I am still learning and getting fiercer. I remember my first audition. I was a mess!!

I did, "Toxic" by Britney (and boy was it toxic).

I was horrible; my nerves got the best of me, though I had been on stage in musicals and theatre.

My friend Pearl said, "Well you are pretty, but you have no rhythm. You need to work on your stage presence."

I thought I was going to die. I kept working. My next audition included the song, "If You Could Read My Mind." I did a little better, but I still was not quite there. I felt glamorous in my coral gown and white fur wrap.

Once again Pearl said, "You are gorgeous, but you really have no rhythm!"

I did not expect that again. Pearl hated me. She would read my friend Rachael and I because we would go to the club half-naked (and we were not a size three).

I remember New Year's Eve at Revolutions in Orlando 2008. I met Bob Taylor. He was a legend in the DRAG world. He told me I was gorgeous. I never saw myself like that before. People told me I was pretty, but here is someone well known, practically a celebrity in his own right telling me I was pretty.

That was a turning point for me; I wanted to be my best. I kept working on my looks to perfect the image I needed to portray on stage. Eventually I got close to Bob and he said I should be London Taylor, because at the time I did not have a last name. I was hesitant and told him this because there are like a million Taylors and I was not sure if I wanted to be in such a large family.

I thought about all the gorgeous women and men that made up the Taylors; I was sold. They were such a talented group of people I could not think of any other family I would rather be.

A little more down the road, I was still performing and working the dressing room. One night a gorgeous tall blonde-haired woman came into the dressing room. She had the elegance of a goddess, but the attitude of a young vibrant woman.

She was Dana Douglas. I will admit I was a little intimidated by her. I had no idea who she was. I asked Pearl and she explained that Dana was a former Miss Continental and so much more. Somehow, Dana and I started getting closer. We realized our similarities, our love of performing, and the love of a normally fulfilled life.

Dana and Bob were close. It was great to know such amazing people. Not just from the DRAG perspective, but they are truly amazing people. So here I am today as London Taylor Douglas. So grateful for my journey, entertainment wise as well as my personal life. It has been an adventure and this is only the beginning. I will continue to push the envelope, try different things, and improve as much as I can.

London Taylor Douglas

A good teacher is a master of simplification and an enemy of simplism.

Louis A. Berman

Saluting

Carmella Marcella Garcia

❀❀❀ *with limited editing* ❀❀❀

In the world of female impersonation, everyone knows only a few names. As a former Miss Gay Universe, Miss Gay USofA at Large, Miss Continental Plus, Miss Gay Florida America, and so many other grand titles, "The Grand Ole' Gal of the South" is one of the giants. Her fans know her as Carmella Marcella Garcia. To me, she is mama.

Somehow, in my early days of starting DRAG, Carmella saw something in me when she took me under her wing to become my DRAG mother. She has performed professionally for over twenty five years all over the country to the amazement of audiences, and seen thousands of DRAG queens, yet she has only selected a few to nurture and call her children. Therefore, I am very blessed, especially as she chose me; I did not ask her to be my DRAG mother.

Carmella was responsible for teaching me the art of impersonation via DRAG pageant interviewing techniques, evening gown modeling, and accessorizing an outfit "DRAG style."

Where others had shown me how they put makeup on their own faces, he taught me the "how and why" of each element to produce highlights or contours under a stage light. He taught me how to blend a wig line along with the basics of styling a wig. I heard other DRAG queens talk of their DRAG mother and what little they actually taught them, there were no guessing games with Carmella. If I did not know, I was to ask, and she would help me.

Beyond the elements of DRAG, Carmella also invited me into the life of his male persona. In female impersonation, we often keep our male lives very separate from our female lives. We often do not let our "DRAG" friends meet our "real" friends.

Carmella made me a part of that life too. I have been to his home numerous times including Thanksgiving dinner, met his mother, and spent time in theme parks like Disney and Universal together hanging out. He not only made me a part of his DRAG family, but a part of his inner family.

My favorite memory with Carmella was when she renamed me in the world of DRAG. When I started, I had chosen the name Christi Lowe. Some told me that I sounded like a little girl rather than a true entertainer, so I needed a grander name. I changed it to Christina Lowe but people repeated it was too simple of a name, so I changed it to Christina Alexandria Lowe.

Through it all, Carmella did her best to keep up, announcing me to audiences with each name change. The night I gave up Miss Gay Florida

America, Carmella was emceeing. It was time for my final number, but she had no idea who was up next.

In typical Carmella humor she said, "Up next is a fantastic entertainer. Who is up next?" She was told it was me. Then she said "Oh yes! A fantastic entertainer. What name is she going by this week? Oh screw it! Ladies and Gentlemen, welcome to the stage your current reigning Miss Gay Florida America, Christina Alexandria Victoria Regina Lowenstein the third! And if she don't like it, tough $h!t!"

I have since chosen to drop the "nstein the third" portion, but have affectionately kept the rest of the gift my mama chose for me, making me by her words, "The Grandest Name in Female Impersonation."

She told me later; no one can give me any more grief about my name not being grand enough for the world of DRAG.

Being protective is something Carmella takes very seriously with her DRAG children. She is just like a mother hen; you do not hurt her kids. She will come to their defense to defend their honor in a New York minute. She has even done this with me, to which I am very thankful.

DRAG queens can be a vicious lot and gossip, rumors, and vendettas can run rampant, but Carmella is a name most know and respect. One does not want to cross her and get on her bad side. Thus, when Carmella speaks, people listen. When Carmella's protective mode kicks in, you feel safe and know everything will be alright.

Carmella Marcella Garcia took a boy who dressed in women's clothes and taught him how to be a female impersonator and a DRAG queen. She truly changed my life for the better. Her tag line is "Grand Ole' Gal of the South," and on stage, she is grand. With me, she is nothing but humble, caring, protective, and loving. It has been a gift for me to know this wonderful man; my mentor, teacher, counselor, and friend.

All of my love to George Timothy Reed, the man behind my DRAG mother, Carmella Marcella Garcia.

Christina Alexandria Victoria Regina Lowe

"Seldom was any knowledge given to keep, but to impart; the grace of this rich jewel is lost in concealment."

Bishop Hall

Saluting

Vaunessa Vale, Vicki Dominatrix,
And Lana Davis

❀ ❀ ❀ with limited editing ❀ ❀ ❀

I found my mentors in the fast-paced world of DRAG pageantry. They influenced my growth in the art form. Each, in their own way, served as a role model, teacher, and inspiration to me. Among those words I value the most are the following quotes,

Vaunessa Vale: "Never, never give up."

Lana Davis: "It is not what every other queen is doing that matters, it is more important that you be yourself,"

Vicki Dominatrix: "In this art form, reputation is everything."

Bianca DeMonet

Unedited excerpts from the files of the
Number one selling book on this craft,

❀ Original DRAG Handbook ❀

These messages were shared in the questionnaire posted to create the book's vibe, content, and character. Pardon the English. Many confessed later that they filled out the forms after returning from the bars.

Raquel Payne

There are so many amazing and beautiful queens out there that have the biggest hearts. They will help you in any way they can. There are also many bitter queens who feel like everyone is a threat and trying to take their spot at a club or they are after their title. I'm lucky enough to be surrounded by loving queens who are supportive and have become my best friends.

Nairobi D'Viante

There are people who support me and I always make sure to be on my best to make them proud.

"He that teaches us anything which we knew not before is undoubtedly to be reverenced as a master."

Samuel Johnson

Saluting

Anita Mann

❀❀❀ *with limited editing* ❀❀❀

Dear Anita Mann,

It's funny that, even though there is more distance between us than has ever been before, I could still not feel any closer to you. You inspire, inform, and sometimes intimidate me with your understanding of the landscape of gay life. I know that you have saved my life in more ways than you will ever know.

I still remember the first time that I met you. You had recently returned from back-up dancing with Tasha Nicole at USofA. You choreographed and organized most of her talent that trip...there isn't a girl from the "real" Illinois that could succeed with you. You're always so graciously available. I had just begun sneaking into the bar weeks before we met.

We met when I was brought backstage to see the show cast at the Club. I was in awe and struck with fear. This was the gay life I had been waiting to see, since I was caught with gay porn in high school. I was so unprepared, as I tried to find a seat in the crowded dressing room so I could catch a breath.

Without pausing or looking away from your mirror, you quickly responded, "If you're looking for a place to sit down, you could always try my face."

You were bold and smiling. I was terrified and shaking. I think we both started laughing.

I remember the long talks we had backstage or on car trips. I will never forget the sage advice that flowed from your mouth like lyrics from some favorite Missy Elliot song.

You were right. They were freaks on the hunt to take what they could. You told me the safe way to say no and the safer ways to say yes. You helped me see the gay community for more than just good times and fast goodbyes.

Many people criticize the gay community for being against family values, but you taught me that the value of a family sometimes means just sitting with friends. Sometimes you can choose your family. You can love them, look out for them, cheerlead, fight then make-up, support, lead, trust, disappoint, surprise, and be loved by them. You complicated my life by challenging what I think and do.

I remember the first time you put me in DRAG for the Miss Newcomer Illinois pageant. I think I found sixty ways to tell you no without hurting your feelings. You found sixty-one ways to ask me to just try. You wore me down. I think that was always your goal. I agreed to try DRAG one time.

You figured out the loophole and demanded it be at a pageant for which you would provide everything. I remember having this fear that my life was about to change. I somehow convinced myself that this would be a one-time thing. I think you knew better.

You were right. I somehow stumbled my way into the crown that night in a pair of heels. I can honestly say that was the first time in my life I had ever even tried a pair on. In a matter of hours, you had me spinning, flipping, and chasing my wig all over the stage.

I remember the last time you asked me to do DRAG. Your voice was soft and unsure. It did not match what I knew of you at all. You told me about getting your tonsils out and scared me with what they found. When you asked if the last request you ever made could be me entering the Miss Gay Illinois USofA pageant. You had never really asked me about anything. I knew I couldn't say no. Who would have guessed?

Miracles are possible. I just cannot figure out which is the greater miracle: the fact that you made a full recovery or the fact that I won another unintended crown.

I'll tell you what has been miraculous for me. I found someone who loves, supports, and accepts me...not in spite of who I am...but because of who I am. I know that I will never be able to return even an ounce of what you have given me. You are fierce! You know you cannot be touched on the stage, but I want you to know that you have made an impact off the stage as well. You changed me. I will always love you.

Bryan "Critiqa Mann" Asbury

**"The greatest sign of success for a teacher
is to be able to say,
The children are now working
as if I did not exist."**

Maria Montessori

 **Original DRAG Handbook** 

These messages were shared in the questionnaire posted to create the book's vibe, content, and character. Pardon the English. Many confessed later that they filled out the forms after returning from the bars.

Trixie LaRue

Entertaining is definitely not something I could do alone. Even if I dressed, costumed, and painted myself I need that DJ to hit play and at least that one audience member to support me.

Jade Daniels

I've only ever known our community to be very supportive and helpful to newcomers. And I don't think anyone could make it anywhere in any business without the help of others.

**"Be careful to leave your sons well instructed rather
than rich, for the hopes of the instructed are better
than the wealth of the ignorant."**

Epictetus

Saluting

Champale Denise

❀❀❀ with limited editing ❀❀❀

Just saying her name conjures up images of beauty and grace. She always carries herself with such elegance. Champale was always the life of the party and she still is. Whether she knew it or not, she is one of the few queens that cult vated who I am today!

Champale taught me to be comfortable with myself, to have fun on stage, give the crowd what they want, but still be who you are!

She is the ultimate emcee, hosting pageants or one of her shows at The Carousel II in Knoxville, Tennessee. She includes the crowd into her performances with her "uhhhs." She brings people on stage and breaks it down.

Around Champale you always feel special; like you belong. She never degrades you or makes you feel inferior. Instead, she remembers what it is like in the beginning and is willing to offer her assistance.

Now with all that said, don't expect some prissy little Barbie. Don't get me wrong, Champale is beautiful and she can be a lady. She is a mix between "the best friend you used to smoke pot with under the bleachers and the older sister willing to show you the way!"

PurrZsa Kyttyn

"Teaching is not a lost art,
but the regard for it is a lost tradition."

Jacques Barzun

Saluting

Tattianna Delarouge
and Justin Barnes Williams

❀❀❀ *with limited editing* ❀❀❀

When my own family kicked me out in the middle of winter, they took me in. They were the ones who loved and supported me when my biological family would not support me. I think sometimes that the love and support from friends makes them family even if the blood is different.

Thank you to Justin Barnes Williams and Tattianna Delarouge being the best parents anyone could ask for!

Jazmen Andrews

Unedited excerpts from the files of the
Number one selling book on this craft,

❀ Original DRAG Handbook ❀

These messages were shared in the questionnaire posted to create the book's vibe, content, and character. Pardon the English. Many confessed later that they filled out the forms after returning from the bars.

Conundrum
I do believe that I would not be where I am today without being blessed with the people I have in my life. I am very thankful everyday knowing I have a great group of friends and family standing behind every decision I have decided to make. They keep me grounded and show me right from wrong as well as helping me with things that I had no experience.

Rusti Fawcett
<Rusti loves the CAP key too.> I OWE MISS P EVERYTHING I KNOW ABOUT COMEDIC TIMING AND FOR BEING THE BEST TO MY DRAG MOM. I OWE THE PARLIAMENT HOUSE FOR SEEING I HAD A TALENT AND GIVING ME MY FIRST JOB AND CARMELLA MARCELLA GARCIA FOR LIBERATING ME IN THE 80'S SHE'LL NO WHAT THAT MEANS.

"A master can tell you what he expects of you. A teacher though, awakens your own expectations."

Patricia Neal

Saluting

**Mokha Montrese and
Alonzo Ceapriola-Williams**

❀❀❀ *with limited editing* ❀❀❀

I can honestly say both of my parents I love very much; I never thought I would have made it this far until they came into my life. Both of them have encouraged me to keep going for my dreams, to believe in myself, and keep striding for whatever I believe my heart has sent me. Without them teaching me the "do's and don'ts" I would have actually failed and given up on what I believe I am great at doing and love so much. I have the honor of having legends in my life that have passed something great to me.

AJ Allen

There are hundreds of performers, which lead their lives with their heart. They are the mentors that reach out to hold their hand, to hug them when they cry, to share in their laughter, to motivate and to inspire. Very few performers seek to be that person, and it is sad. Those people will transform their art.

A passage from the Official DRAG Handbook
DRAG411.com

 Original DRAG Handbook

These messages were shared in the questionnaire posted to create the book's vibe, content, and character. Pardon the English. Many confessed later that they filled out the forms after returning from the bars.

Beverly LaSalle

I have had a number of people that have either helped me, or wanted to see me succeed. Dana Douglas gave me my first big break. Mis Sadistic helped me develop and blossom into who I am today, along with countless friends and venues that have done everything to help me get to where I am today. I thank and love you all!

Anastasia Rexia

We have all been helped either directly or indirectly. We take influence and trailblazers for granted. There are people out there who opened doors for you.

Jade Jolie

I've been helped by many incredible entertainers. I think this is so nice to be able to recognize them. Miss Siren, Lashes from Metro in Jacksonville, Lady Pearl, Juwanna Jackson, Vanessa Moore, Kelcy Divine from the University Club in Gainesville and Dana Douglas from FL. I know there are so many more that has inspired me with their help but these ladies just stick out in my mind dearly.

Kitty D'Meaner

I learn from others. I learn by watching others. Some of the same people inspire me, on and off the stage. Some of them have helped me personally, and others just by watching them perform. Either way, I am truly blessed to have these people in my life, and to be able to work with them on a regular basis. I would not be where I am without the support and guidance of these people.

Stephen Brooks

You learn from the best, and ya learn from the WORST!! But, most of us are surrounded by our sisters, that to pick out one or two is tough!!!

❀ Original DRAG Handbook ❀

These messages were shared in the questionnaire posted to create the book's vibe, content, and character. Pardon the English. Many confessed later that they filled out the forms after returning from the bars.

Barbra Seville

Drag is competitive and constantly evolving, as is technology and acceptance. Some people will feel cheated that they could not read a book like this. Others (like me) hate that new queens go to "you-tube" to copy a good routine instead of creating one.

Curtis Vegas Wixey

I have had struggles throughout my time in this industry, like we all have, and have at times felt like i was all alone in my endeavors. And the truth of the matter is, i did this all on my own, and of course there was help alon the way, and i picked things up as the years went on, but it was me who pushed me to be the best me i can be. I credit many people with helping me along that way though!

Saluting

**Alexis De La Mer, Makayla Rose Devine,
Amanda Bone DeMornay, Sasha Sensation, and Freeda Bone**

❀❀❀ *with limited editing* ❀❀❀

Alexis De La Mer gave me my first taste of real DRAG. She helped me in so many ways, and I thank her from the bottom of my heart.

Makayla Rose Devine gave me tips and helped me through so much.

Amanda Bone DeMornay took me in and helped me get my shit together. She showed me how to paint and pad like a queen. She also gave me the chance to be part of an awesome cast at Valentines. Amanda does more for me than anyone. I am so, so, so very thankful for her.

Sasha Sensation and Freeda Bone helped me tremendously by giving me pointers to become a fierce queen.

I would be so lost without all of you. I have such love and support around me. Thank you all for being kind hearted queens.

TotiYanah Diamond

Top Ten History's Greatest Teachers

Even the Greatest of Teachers began with one simple hope to make a difference

Confucius
(551-479 B.C.E.)

Confucius was a Chinese teacher and philosopher who preached the values of formal learning. He taught thousands of students during his lifetime, focusing on what he termed the Six Arts; these include music, archery, mathematics, ritual, chariot-riding and calligraphy. Additionally, Confucius placed a strong emphasis on morals and integrity. His influence as a teacher shaped Chinese education for several millennia and has impacted education and philosophy throughout the world.

**"Ideal teachers are those
who use themselves as bridges over which they
invite their students to cross, then having facilitated
their crossing, joyfully collapse, encouraging them
to create bridges of their own."**

Nikos Kazantzakis

Saluting

D' Marco Knight

❀❀❀ *with limited editing* ❀❀❀

I have to say growing up in a small country town of Coal Grove, Ohio where everyone was in a time warp, interracial couples and gay couples are hated. I grew up in a family of respect and love. My mom battled cancer for fifteen years, raising me to be who I wanted to be in life.

My first pageant I had the chance to watch my DRAG parent and brother Aj Allen compete for Mr. Stonewall 2010. I messaged him on facebook and the adventure began when he told me I could be whoever I wanted to be.

I was raised in a gay family. My mom, her brother Sable Knight (the DRAG queen originally from Huntington, West Virginia), and myself fought for everything.

Aj became my inspiration. He took me under his wing and gave me tips, respect, and love. He truly has my heart in friendship. I was so nervous the first time I performed. I felt I needed to call him. He told me not to be nervous and to be myself.

I am proud to call AJ Allen my DRAG parent because he truly inspired me to keep going. Aj Allen will always be in my heart. I look up to him in every way. He has done so much in my life. I use to be shy, and felt useless,

Aj is someone you can chat with to make you feel great about yourself.

D' Marco Knight

**"A teacher's purpose
is not to create students in his
own image, but to develop students
who can create their own image."**

Author Unknown

❀ Original DRAG Handbook ❀

These messages were shared in the questionnaire posted to create the book's vibe, content, and character. Pardon the English. Many confessed later that they filled out the forms after returning from the bars.

Wendy G. Kennedy

I began my journey at Starlight By The Park and The Golden Lantern, I've performed at OZ and John Paul's Bar and I'm a guest at The Appletini Revue and The Society page, all of them in New Orleans. I love Miss Toebe, Miss Marcy Marcell for booking me, also Miss Dee and Stephanie, Mercedes Ellis delorean, Jaded Jay, just to name a few…However I must thank Raven Kennedy (My Drag Mom), Monica Synclair (my Drag Sister) for believing in me. all my Queens have won Tiaras and they have helped me along the way and continue to do so. Last but not least Tye the Boss Marshal and my wife, who supports my efforts to become the best I can be.

Wendal Duppert

It's all in your approach and attitude. I've found an AMAZING community of talented, caring gay men. If you're only "in it to win it" you're going to be pretty lonely. If you're enjoying the journey, are a little less self-centered and a little more giving, all of the right people will come into your life.

Aurora Sexton

If you don't remember where you came from and the people that got you there, you are destined for failure. No one likes a diva and being an entertainer in many cases is a team effort, ESPECIALLY in pageantry. I don't know where I would be without the belief and support of some amazing people and venues who have aided my career so to those of you that did, Thank you!

Saluting

Connie Lickus and
Butch Harry Lickus

❀❀❀ *with limited editing* ❀❀❀

Q: She's tall, amazing, gives great advice, supports me and much more. Who is the she I am referring to in this statement?

A: My DRAG mom Connie Lickus (along with her hunky husband, my dad Butch Harry Lickus).

I do not know how my DRAG parents met, but by the pictures online I'm sure it was a bar's back room. Connie is always there to help anyone starting out or already in the DRAG world. She has provided everything to amateurs on nights when they forget things. She tells you "like she sees it."

If you look funny, something is off, or she dislikes your song, she will let you know. At the same time, she supports you. She backs you up even if you are country, hip-hop, or rock and roll. I love going to watch my mom perform, even with her black and purple hair.

I hope she knows she will always have me to support her. She can go out any night and rock any outfit to any song choice. I hope you have a chance in your busy, hectic crazy life to see her perform.

Jake Lickus

"If you think education is expensive, try ignorance."

Andy McIntyre

Saluting

Ray and Raphael Matthews

❀❀❀ *with limited editing* ❀❀❀

I started performing male entertainment in 2006. Ray and Raphael Matthews for the Mr. Gay USA Nationals adopted me. I strive to be like them some day and to accomplish the goals they have set for me. Arabia Knight-Addams took me under her wing and taught me the true meaning of performance. I owe my success to Arabia, Ray, and Raphael if it wasn't for you I wouldn't be who I am today. Much love and happiness and remember Don't H8.

Chip Matthews

Saluting

Aj Allen

❀❀❀ *with limited editing* ❀❀❀

Dear AJ,

I want to say I love you from the bottom of my heart. You are an amazing man and I look up to you so much. I cannot even begin to put into words, how thankful and blessed I am to have the chance to know you and call you family. You are always and forever my "Big Mama."

You have been such a huge source of joy, laughter, love, and inspiration. I honestly don't know what I would do without your presence in my life. You have given me a great role model to look up to (and to try to be like).

The amount of respect I have for you cannot be put into words. I don't think you will ever realize the impression and affect you have had on me and my life. It is weird to think I have only known you for such a short amount of time, and yet you have made such a huge impact on me.

You are one of the very few people that has shown me what it looks like to stay true to yourself. You are without any apologies or fears. This is something I have always admired about you. You possess the ability to look at adversity and criticism in the face, and basically smile and brush it all off.

I have to admit, writing this was harder than I thought. It is difficult to put into words the way I feel about you. I look forward to a spending my life with you as a friend. No matter where life takes us, where we end up, I will always have you in my heart as a close dear friend, whom I love greatly.

I am so very, very, very proud to call you my Father. I am honored to be a part of the legacy that is the Montrese family.

Mirage Montrese

"Treat people as if they were what they ought to be and you help them become what they are capable of becoming."

Goethe

Saluting

Alexis Principle

❀❀❀ *with limited editing* ❀❀❀

St. Louis, Missouri.

My DRAG mother, the first time I watched her perform I got chills because of her total illusion, entertainment value, gorgeousness, and talent!

Her stage presence overwhelmed me!

I could not believe it was a man. Most of all, she inspired me. The perfection in the transformation was amazing. She is why I am a female impersonator today. I have the utmost respect for my craft and this industry!

India Starr Simms

 Original DRAG Handbook 

These messages were shared in the questionnaire posted to create the book's vibe, content, and character. Pardon the English. Many confessed later that they filled out the forms after returning from the bars.

BukkakeBlaque London St James

The learning curve is all over the place and yes you will learn from everyone. However where I am from you are fed to the wolves until you can show that you are in it to win it. You need to have thick skin and suffer for a bit then they will give you pointers. I am still relatively new to the art of drag and have gained a lot of ground by just watching a picking apart other queens. Taking the good the bad and the ugly and trying to make it work for you is what it is all about. Once the makeup was under control other queens started to step in and be helpful with tips and blending secrets that I had no clue about. I have been performing for eight months and I only really had help in the last 2 months so after that long comment. I would say everyone for themselves. Good Luck to all and I will help if I can.

Barbra Herr

I was fortunate to have met Antonio Pantojas in the seventies in Puerto Rico. He was the drag entertainer of mainstream on the island...he took me under his wing and is STILL my dear friend to this day..

Saluting

Candi Stratton

❀❀❀ *with limited editing* ❀❀❀

I would like to start this letter by saying you are simply divine! So many people strive to be the very thing you are, the true definition of class, beauty, poise, talent, and exceptional character all rolled into one! I only hope you understand how much of an inspiration you are not only to me, but to many people. On behalf of all of them, I thank you!

You are so much more than you will ever know. I would like to thank you for all you have already done for me, and all you will do for me in the future. Like you, I felt lost at a point in my career. I felt I didn't have a place and I never really fit in. It seemed like every door shut in my face. I noticed sometimes even friends and sisters turning their backs on me. I stayed strong for so long and came to a point where I felt that maybe it just is not worth the hassle. I heard you say the words I have longed to hear my whole life "Jade, I love you."

You amazed me by taking me under your guidance and allowing me to take one of the most prestigious names in the business, Stratton! As my mother, you gave me the best advice, ideas, support, and guidance. Most importantly, you give me love. Not fake love or a one of pretentiousness. I feel no matter where you are in the world, from Switzerland, Las Vegas, or Colorado, you always brightened my life. I have truly reflected on my own actions and now find myself asking if each action I take would make you proud, or if it is something you would approve.

This alone makes me a better person. I look at each day with a positive attitude and in return, this makes me much better! I

I sit here in tears writing this letter, knowing that someone with no biological connection can love me so much. Every single day I am blessed and humbled to know that regardless if I win a crown, put on a great show, or paint for the gods, I can always look over my shoulder and know you are never far behind smiling at me blowing a kiss and simply loving me!

There are times in our lives where great things happen and we tend to be caught in our own drama and life. We forget to acknowledge the blessing that has entered our life! I have always been a firm believer that nothing is an accident and everything happens for a reason, sometimes not as fast as you may want them to happen, but in due time will happen.

Candi happened to me and I want to take this time to truly say from the bottom of my heart CANDI STRATTON aka MOMMY DEAREST, "I love you with every ounce of love I have to give. I appreciate you for everything you are now and will be in my life! When I look back at my life, if I become just half the person you are... I have succeeded. You are everything and I love you because you love me!

Jade S. Stratton

Saluting

India Divine

❀❀❀ *with limited editing* ❀❀❀

My DRAG mother is India Divine, from Bowling Green, Kentucky. I have about ten DRAG sisters including, Telishis Jackson and Monai Divine.

India has kept us together through trials and tribulations, drama, and heartaches. She is truly a good person at heart, and has helped us become the queens we are today. She has poked us, prodded, painted, soothed, and gave us hell from time to time. What she does is all in the name of love. I would like to thank her for all her help

Emerald Divine

Top Ten History's Greatest Teachers

Even the Greatest of Teachers began with one simple hope to make a difference

Socrates
(469-399 B.C.E.)

Socrates is considered one of Western Civilization's most significant teachers and philosophers. He led discussions with the people of Athens in which he posed challenging and profound questions. Though he refused payment for his teaching, Socrates engendered fierce loyalty among his students. One of his students, Plato, would go on to become another major figure in the history of Western philosophy. His style of stimulating thought through question asking has been adopted by many modern teachers and is known as the Socratic method.

"I think a hero is an ordinary individual who finds strength to persevere and endure in spite of overwhelming obstacles."

Christopher Reeve

Saluting

Lori Ashley Williams

❀❀❀ *with limited editing* ❀❀❀

Talented, beautiful, caring, loving, funny, stern, honest, the ultimate Patti LaBelle Impersonator.

These are a few words to describe my DRAG mother, and I would not be alone. I learned from her the art of performing, having stage presence, class, hair, make up, sewing, stepping out of my comfort zone, and the complete art of DRAG.

She was never afraid to take risks.

"Life is a stage, just make sure you're in the spotlight every chance you get baby," she always said to me.

She was not only influential to me, but she is the driving force. She passed away in 1998, but her spirit is always with me. It pushes me harder every day to LIVE, LOVE and LAUGH. All of the gifts she blessed me with made me the person and entertainer I am today.

I am, and will always be, forever grateful. I love and miss you momma.

Elysse Giovanni

"If a seed of a lettuce will not grow, we do not blame the lettuce. Instead, the fault lies with us for not having nourished the seed properly."

Buddhist proverb

Top Ten History's Greatest Teachers

Even the Greatest of Teachers began with one simple hope to make a difference

Roger Bacon
(c. 1214-1292)

A native of England, Roger Bacon was a friar and scholar in many academic areas, including mathematics, early chemistry and optics. He conducted experiments that greatly advanced the understanding of philosophy and science in his day. His advocacy of Aristotle, as well as many of his other academic pursuits, caused conflict with some religious leaders. His outspoken teaching and writing style led to an imprisonment of nearly fifteen years and later accusations of occultism.

Saluting

**Britney Halston
and Erick McCray**

❀❀❀ with limited editing ❀❀❀

I began doing DRAG shows in January of 1998. I didn't have much guidance or direction until I started doing shows with the person that is now my DRAG mother Britney Halston.

Before I became her daughter, she would say to me, "I really like how you did this, but next time use something like this or try doing something like that."

I took her advice and she saw me grow not only as an entertainer, but as a DRAG queen as well. When I became her DRAG daughter, I joined a big family that cared not just about DRAG, but also more importantly, being a family.

Fortunately, I was raised in a DRAG family that taught the old values of DRAG. It is not about how much money you make or the price of your costumes, it is about entertaining, making someone smile, laugh or cry. It's about putting your heart on your sleeve and putting every emotion you have in each and every performance.

Treat people with respect and kindness and no matter how someone looks, they are always beautiful.

Britney Halston and her husband Erick have been my DRAG parents since I started in 1998. They taught me the meaning of the words "true family." We do not have to be blood to be family. They love me with unconditional love that still to this day… amazes me.

There isn't a holiday or birthday that goes by where we don't call one another, or a lonely depressed night that I can't call, no matter what time, just to talk or cry.

My biological father was gone since I was sixteen. My DRAG father Erick filled that void and provided me with the love, compassion, direction, and guidance that a father should show his kids.

Britney and Erick have shaped my life way beyond expression. There are no words to ever begin to show them the absolute love and respect that I have for them. I would not be the entertainer or person I am today. They gave me the courage to do the things that I have done in my career without the encouragement of my DRAG parents, Britney Halston and Erick McCray. We are, and always will be, a true family!

Vanity Halston

Saluting

Rachael Sommers

❀ ❀ ❀ with limited editing ❀ ❀ ❀

There have been so many people that affected my life as it pertains to the art of female impersonation, but none more so than Rachael Sommers.

I know him as Robbie, my partner of thirteen years. He is hands down one of the most talented people I have ever met in my life. When we met, I was so naïve I had no idea what a DRAG queen or transsexual even was. I was fresh off the farm as they say.

When he told me he liked to do DRAG, and consequently briefed me on what it was, I was entirely open minded (having not had the chance yet to be warped by stereotypes that so often occur in our community). I thought it was interesting, fun and colorful. I told Robbie if he liked doing it, that he should. He was amazed I was so open to it and so we both grew together as creative individuals, Robbie the entertainer, and me as a college student and scenic photographer.

One summer day in 2003, he needed a headshot for Rachael and begged me to take it. I didn't want to, because I didn't know how to properly photograph people, or so I thought. He said it didn't matter and to just try, and so I did. That headshot was the beginning of what became Kristofer Reynolds Photography. Together with my eye and her creative ingenuity, we have shot almost every major entertainer in our genre over the past eight years.

Thank you Robbie for taking my hand in life, guiding me through all the ugliness, and capturing the beauty that is in it. I love you.

Kristofer Reynolds

"Learning is finding out what we already know. Doing is demonstrating that you know it. Teaching is reminding others that they know just as well as you. You are all learners, doers, and teachers."

Richard Bach

Saluting

Dr. J

❃❃❃ *with limited editing* ❃❃❃

Dr. J is my DRAG Daddy. I am blessed to have him as my mentor. I was toying with the idea of performing for a few years, but he was my inspiration and backbone to do it!

He surprised me by coming to a fashion show I was competing in for charity, and decided I had to perform with him. He spent countless hours with me on the phone, suggesting wardrobes, songs, and dress rehearsal to ensure we didn't have a costume faux pas!

Dr. J was relentless in helping me attempt to act masculine on stage. Girly kicks, flick of the wrist, ohhhhhhhh and that walk!

He still lovingly calls me Popeye!

The main thing was, "Know your words!!"

Every breath, hesitation, a lift of the eyebrow...

The time Dr. J invested in me all in the first week alone was staggering. We had our first performance a week later. I did a comedy number, country song, and a duet with my Daddy. The comedy was okay and the country song gave me problems.

The number we did together was my favorite. The time and patience he spent with me to build my confidence, picking me up when I wanted to quit, and the numerous cups of coffee we drank proved the faith he had in me!

When the performances were well received, I thought I could breathe, but, NOOOOO!

That was just the beginning. Daddy gave me a not so soft nudge for a talent contest. With his direction, I won.

Thought I could breathe the following week after I performed for winning, NOT!!

Three weeks to the day, after my first performance, I was nudged into a pageant. The continuous phone conversations (because we lived an hour and a half away from each other), the numerous e-mails with revisions to my introduction speech, and, many more pots of coffee, I entered.

Who do you think was my dresser?

Absolutely, Dr. J!

I had a creative red costume complete with red beard for presentation, that he made sure I didn't look like a complete idiot wearing, followed by a quick wardrobe change costume for talent part of the pageant,

I was a complete wreck, but my Daddy put his hands on my face, looked me square in the eyes and said,

"Vinnie, breathe. You have this; we practiced. I'll get you a drink!"

I know you all are thinking we had that mandatory shot. I got news for you "I do not drink." I did however; get a nice, fresh, hot cup of coffee!

I am the new kid on the block at forty-nine years old, winning a crown. The best part of the win was when daddy came up to tip me, when I did my crowning song, he hugged me so tight he darn near lifted me off my feet (and I'm bigger than him).

He continues to guide and coach me like any dad would help his son with baseball. Even though he is semi-retired, he still makes it to my shows, encourages me when needed, and can still give me a swift kick, too!!

I love you Dr. J!

Vinnie Marconi

"Bitter are the roots of study,
but how sweet their fruit."

Cato

Saluting
Tova Uravitch
❀❀❀ *with limited editing* ❀❀❀

I cannot honestly think of a more caring and compassionate person on the face of the planet. I decided in late 2007 after going to my first show that DRAG was for me. I loved it, because I saw the limits pushed by one entertainer...Tova Uravitch.

I sat there in awe of her costuming, makeup, and hair. It was fierce, which was not a word in my vocabulary until she stepped on the stage. Like all beginners, I looked a mess. Eyebrows up to my hairline, some Covergirl eyeshadow, and after a few months with a DRAG mother that didn't try to help me, I called my friend Tova.

It was the first time I had to do my makeup by myself. She walked me through everything, step by step, over the phone.

Keep in mind, she was working her boy job in Pennsylvania at the time and I was a struggling boy in a dress in Kentucky, that she did not have to help, but she took the time to do so. A few weeks later, my name was changed. I was now Uravitch and have remained so ever since.

Tova gives with her heart. She helps other people before herself and yet she still has time to inspire newcomers and captivate audiences everywhere she goes. For someone who has never really seen themselves as a role model or mentor to the community, she's made one hell of a name for herself!

Akasha Uravitch

"Education is not the filling of a pail
but the lighting of a fire."

William Butler Yeats

Saluting

**Alyssa Williams, Bob Taylor,
Chelsea Pearl and her husband Marcus**

❀❀❀ *with limited editing* ❀❀❀

I am very fortunate to have a good DRAG family. I have had two DRAG mothers and two DRAG fathers. Let's start with the moms:

My first mother is Alyssa Williams. She was the one that sat me down and showed me the things I needed to paint my face. She gave me the instructions to create my current abilities.

Chelsea Pearl is my second DRAG mother. She took me under her wing and I could not be more thankful. Her grace and art form is amazing that is recognized nationwide. She is one of my idols and icons. I love learning from her. She has the power to capture our attentions with just her grace and face.

Marcus is Chelsea's husband. He took me under his wing and has coached me in my personal life.

Mr. Bob Taylor is my second father; his knowledge in the industry is nationally well known. Being a Taylor is a privilege. Bob's persona is respected all around in the nation.

Adriana Fuentes

"There are two kinds of people; those who do the work and those who take the credit. Try to be in the first group; there is less competition there."

Indira Gandhi

Saluting

**Amirage and
Robbi Lynn**

❀❀❀ *with limited editing* ❀❀❀

My one and only mother is Amirage, a living legend, great entertainer, as well as a role model. She has been in my life since I began my

DRAG career as Erykah Mirage. She passed many great skills to me and my sibling including makeup tips, hair, clothing, and accessories. Amirage is also a well-known role model in the LGBT Community. She shows the community that it does not stop within the community; we must keep our heads held high and go for whatever we set our minds to. Whether it be performing on stage to entertain fans or fighting for equal rights for all people. Amirage has a heart of gold and a gift God gave her that shines wherever she goes.

Robbi Lynn is the best mentor, DRAG mother, friend, sister... anybody could ask for. She is one of the legends living today. She helped build the DRAG community and the biggest DRAG show in Kentucky. Robbi appears at many benefit shows, and is truly a "crowd pleaser." She constantly offers a helping hand to those in need, as well as sharing words of wisdom to newcomers. She encouraged my peers and me.

Robbi has a strong mind, a beautiful spirit, and I look forward to continue having her as a close mentor, friend, and family member.

Erykah Mirage

"Every time you wake up and ask yourself, "What good things am I going to do today?" Remember that when the sun goes down at sunset, it takes a part of your life with it." —

Indian proverb

Saluting

Mikaila Natasha Divine

❀❀❀ with limited editing ❀❀❀

In my early career, I had the privilege of formally being adopted by my DRAG mother, Mikaila Natasha Divine. She taught me to stand on my two feet and to put my best foot forward. She always attended my shows in my early days to show me never-ending love and support. When the tough got too tough to handle, she was there to make it easier on me.

We live quite far away from each other. It is always a blessing to see each other. This enables us to reignite the flame of happiness, love, and faith that keeps us strong. I am twenty-five years old, practicing the art of female impersonation for seven years now. I am happy and proud to be in Mikaila's loving DRAG family. We all show love and support for each other.

Felicity Ferraro

Top Ten History's Greatest Teachers

Even the Greatest of Teachers began with one simple hope to make a difference

Jaime Escalante
(1930-2010)

Born in Bolivia, Jaime Escalante taught mathematics at Garfield High School in East Los Angeles, California. Though they had been poor performers, Escalante pushed his students towards success through his dedication, passionate style, and expertise in the material. His tremendous success was significant enough to bring accusations of cheating, though retesting of students proved their capabilities. Edward James Olmos in the 1988 film Stand and Deliver memorably portrayed Escalante.

"To be yourself in a world that is constantly trying to make you something else is the greatest accomplishment."

Ralph Waldo Emerson

Saluting

Amirage Saling

❀❀❀ *with limited editing* ❀❀❀

The year was 1999. Little did I know my life was about to change forever. I ventured out to the local lesbian bar with my girlfriend and a few of our friends to check out a show. Two of my favorite queens were scheduled to perform that evening.

During the show, I saw something I never knew existed, a DRAG king, two of them to be exact. I was floored. From that moment on, I was completely captivated. I didn't know how I was going to make it happen, but I knew I had found the path my life was supposed to take.

Over the years, I made friends with the cast of LaBoy LaFemme at The Connection Night Club. Amirage Saling is a member of that cast. She suggested I enter a talent contest she was hosting one night at Tinkers II.

Her daughter, Aaryn Mirage Payge informed me she was now my DRAG mother and would take me under her wing. I used an Ace bandage to bind my breasts, applied eyeliner, and mascara to my face to imitate facial hair and arrived ready to perform. I had selected the eighties hit Jessie's Girl as my act for the evening. I won first place that night and I will never forget that feeling for the rest of my life. It was pure magic.

Joey Payge

Saluting

Khal Karnage

❀❀❀ *with limited editing* ❀❀❀

I reside in Phoenix, Arizona, and I am a DRAG king. I started doing DRAG on October 25, 2011 at BS West in Scottsdale, Arizona. I was nervous, excited, and anxious. I had never done DRAG before and only been to two DRAG shows before deciding to get it a try.

The bars held none of my other friends that evening because most of my friends were not of age or were busy with other things. Thankfully, two kings in the show were helpful and friendly. I did not get Khal Karnage as a DRAG father until November.

One evening we were both performing at BS West. Khal asked me, "Do you want to be a Karnage?"

I said, "Yes!"

Khal greatly helped me by teaching me to do facial hair and mannerisms to become manlier. He told me to see other DRAG kings to become someone that is different and memorable. I improved as months passed. With his help, support, and love I know that one day I will become something great.

I thank the other DRAG kings and even DRAG queens helping or offering to help me. They have become friends of mine and help me book shows including Felicia K. Minor, Victoria K. Bacon, Ivanna Dooche, Tabatha

Lovall, Crash Bandikok, Ace of Case, Max Richardson, Nikkl Star, Mi$hal De$trange, Ivory Onyx, Jimme Boy Reign, and so many more.

Mentoring also includes thanking Kendra Katoure for having a show at BS West where any DRAG king or queen that is either new or been performing for ages can be in the show. Without you and your show, I would still be wondering what it is like to be a DRAG king. I thank everyone for their love and support.

Vicious Slick

Saluting

Sondra Todd

❁❁❁ *with limited editing* ❁❁❁

Sondra Todd is a name synonymous in Jacksonville, Florida with many things, but above all "Mama." She has been a staple in northeast Florida for over two decades. She has mentored and nurtured more queens and gay youth than most GLBT outreach programs. I met her in 1999 when I decided to perform. It wasn't long before she was taking me under her proverbial wing and guiding me on my way. She had been running her own Talent Search at the Metro for years when I came along.

I was to become part of an extended family including numerous queens, singers, dancers, and friends. Sondra has amazed audiences with her positive attitude, costumes, or emceeing ability. Her quick wit married with her sense of humor and unique way of telling stories left many in stitches. Many entertainers tried to mimic her; including myself. Most of her shows are packed with loyal friends developed from interpersonal relationships over long periods.

Sondra treats her children as her own, sometimes introducing us on the microphone as being born from her mythical womb. She goes above and beyond to make us feel loved, and thought of, and cared for. Not only does she help when needed, but also she is one of the few "mothers" who takes the time to remind us that things are not always easy.

For those of us who live as a part of The House of Todd, it is important to learn where we come from; not just as queens and entertainers, but members of a community often feared and misunderstood. Sondra strives to teach her kids to never take things for granted even when we're riding high; don't forget to nibble on a piece of humble pie. She taught us to respect where we came from, to appreciate the rich diversity of our family, and gay culture. If you are a member of the house of Todd, you know of Sondra's DRAG mother, Carolyn Frye.

As many of us grow into our own and develop our own fans and following, we never stray far from Mama Todd. We are a family first and unity is our bond. When someone is in need, we are on the wire trying to network to pull resources to make small miracles happen. There really isn't much she hasn't taught us to do and when we need her, she is there. One of Sondra's amazing abilities not just as a DRAG mother, but a friend, is to offer subjective advice and sometimes remind us to consider point of views neglected.

She taught us to respect others and ourselves. She inspired us to strive to be our own unique selves. Her love is limitless and her heart knows no boundary. Our house is truly a physical personification of the gay rainbow; many colored and often looked at in awe

Rhiannon Todd

Saluting

Robbi Lynn

❀❀❀ *with limited editing* ❀❀❀

Robbi Lynn (Louisville, KY) has always had this persona of beauty and kindness. In fact, many of us were her children, for she denied no one in providing her assistance. When I was an ugly duckling in the beginning of my career, she took me into her dressing room and groomed me by allowing me to sit with her every Sunday for a year. It was not just makeup and wardrobe for which she prepared me, but of many life lessons as a showgirl and to become a transsexual.

As performers walked the corridors of The Connection dressing rooms, they would jump into Robbi's room to make sure each looked 100% stage ready. If they selected the wrong shoes, she would lend them a pair. If someone's gown were too short, she would pull down a dress from her wardrobe closet to loan. If anyone had questions toward the pathway of becoming transgender, she would sit eye to eye with each girl providing them with all the answers. Robbi Lynn denied nobody.

My mother was teased by the same audience members that ran to her on Halloween to paint them in DRAG; once again she never refused any of them.

Robbi instilled in me, "Always be nice to every person with whom you come into contact."

This is why every person she met over the years still loves and respects her. I owe my career as a performer to my mother. As a mother, she taught me to apply makeup and to understand the purpose of using certain cosmetics in certain areas for the right look. Robbi taught me how to study to represent characters through mannerisms, costumes, and the aura of the characters created. When it came to any of the local pageants, she helped organize my talent numbers.

When I listened to her, I won. When I did not listen, I got the board game version of the show. Robbi always held the pulse to what people wanted to see. As a perfectionist, she taught me how to be one as well. She believed every person in the audience deserved the best entertainment, whether there was one person in the audience or a thousand. I have been so fortunate to call Robbi Lynn my mother. Without her love and commitment as a mother, I would still be doing amateur night both on stage and in life. I love you, Momma!

Amirage Saling

Top Ten History's Greatest Teachers

Even the Greatest of Teachers began with one simple hope to make a difference

Allan Bloom
(1930-1992)

Allan Bloom was a teacher at many schools, including Yale University, Cornell University, and the University of Chicago. He was a leading proponent of the use of the literary canon in education and he worked for many years to influence which books were considered the 'great books' from throughout history. Only through study of these books, Bloom theorized, could an individual contribute to society and understand life in a meaningful way. The books he recommended included ancient texts, such as *Gilgamesh* and Homer's *Iliad*, as well as more modern ones, such as John Steinbeck's *The Grapes of Wrath* and Zora Neale Hurston's *Their Eyes Were Watching God*.

Saluting

Anita Morray

❀❀❀ with limited editing ❀❀❀

I have known Anita Morray for twelve years. For eleven years, he has been my best friend, confidant, and the person teaching me the fundamentals of DRAG. He was originally from the Midwest, while I from New York where we met, we didn't get off on the best foot.

He thought I was the most annoying little twink in the world, and I thought he was an arrogant bitch. It was not long after that I stepped foot onto the stage for the first time. I asked him for advice pursuing DRAG. He 'beat' my face while explaining each step, and then washed it off and made me do it myself!

I was told if I was going to do DRAG I couldn't rely on everyone to do everything for me. With the willingness to learn, and the force of mama, I learned from the ground up. It has always been tough love, but we have been inseparable. I would not ever have it any other way.

Being gay is frowned upon in a Christian-based home, needless to say the desire to be a DRAG queen. My best friend gave me an outlet from negative energy by instilling the talents he had learned over the years into me. He followed in the generations before him. He constantly helped others whom he felt had potential.

I always look to him for his amazing abundance of talents. I was so envious, wanting and waiting for the day when I embodied his talents and stage presence. I have always just wanted to make him proud. After all this time, he still teaches me something new every day. Thank you my mother, my best friend, my mentor.

Tori Sass

Saluting

Sasha Valentino

❀❀❀ with limited editing ❀❀❀

I can remember as if it were yesterday, the first transgender woman I ever met was Sasha Valentino. I was 16 years old and ooooooh boy was I in a state of shock and amazement. I had only seen this type of person on The Jerry Springer show. I was introduced to Sasha in 1996 by my then lover (whom also was a female impersonator) Nina Devaroe.

From the first time I saw Sasha, I knew I wanted to learn more about her and the lifestyle. She intrigued me because I knew she was a man, but looked so much like a woman. She lived like a woman with a straight appearing man.

When I was inducted into the Valentino family, it was not by Sasha Valentino, but her DRAG sister, Stephanie Valentino. Technically this made Sasha my aunt. To my surprise after hanging out and becoming very close to Sasha, she adopted me as her child. My dream of being the child of the legendary Sasha Valentino became reality.

Sasha was my mother, friend, mentor, and pageant teacher. I first attended a DRAG pageant in 1996 Miss Continental where Paris Frantz was crowned. I was so intrigued when I got there to see Sasha. Sasha went from being an ugly duckling to becoming a beautiful swan. Sasha's hard work, dedication, and love she put into her craft and pageant inspired me to compete for the plus size division of Miss Continental Plus. I did not win, but Sasha was so happy and proud of me.

Sasha passed away in December of 2011, and is deeply missed. I love my mother so much and I am forever grateful to her for taking me under her wing. It was such a heartbreaking moment to learn of my mother passing away, but eye opening moment. She will be missed by the world of DRAG and pageantry

I always pay homage to my original DRAG mother Tasha Long. She was the first lady to say, "You are my child." I was once going to be Charisma Long .Tasha and I are still great friends and she is always my mom as well.

Chy'enne Valentino

Saluting

Jerri Lynn

❃ ❃ ❃ with limited editing ❃ ❃ ❃

How blessed I am to think that for thirty-five years I had the pleasure of walking out on stage and performing to countless number of people. None of that would have happened had it not been for my mentor Mr. George Stinson (Jerri Lynn).

Somehow, he saw something in me and took me under his wing. He taught me the difference between being an entertainer and a DRAG queen. It was a much different time when I began. George always knew how to headline a show and it was an honor to work with so many incredible entertainers such as Mickey Day, Dana Christie, Brenda Dee, Lisa St John, Audrey Sinclair, Ethel Waters, Terry Turner, Andora and the Latin Lovely Roxanne.

When people in our part of the country think of the shows, often they assume I speak of the Downtowner on Main Street but actually, they began Chestnut Street that unfortunately was destroyed by fire in 1973. I lost everything in that fire but not my desire for performing. George always had his eye on the next move and that was the Talk of the Town in Newport, Kentucky. Once again, we were in business.

A few gigs later, the new Downtowner opened on Main Street with Jerry Lynn headlining an incredible cast. I was performing at the Mint Julep on 4th Street, but George made room for me to become a regular at the Downtowner in 1975.

Years went on and in true fashion George had his eye on a much bigger prize...When the Downtowner closed in June 1988 George had already opened The Connection. It was a bar like no other around. For the first year we performed on Sundays on the dance floor.

In April 1990 the showroom opened and the rest, as they say, is history. I can only say in closing that in every aspect of my career there was always someone there watching out for me...thank you George...you'll always be my Ruby

Robbi Lynn

Top Ten History's Greatest Teachers

Even the Greatest of Teachers began with one simple hope to make a difference

Nathan Hale
(1755-1766)

Nathan Hale is best known as an American soldier in the Revolutionary War who was captured by the British while acting as a spy. He was hanged at the age of 21, famously saying as his final words, 'I only regret that I have but one life to lose for my country.' He had been a teacher in Connecticut since age 18. He made advances in the cause of providing higher education to women prevented from seeking advanced education, Hale devoted early morning hours to a class of young women learning the same material he would teach their brothers later in the day.

Let us never forget

Please help me fill in the missing names
Of the Official, Orginal DRAG Memorial.

Below is the current list of impersonators no longer with us.
Please go to DRAG411 to view the most current wall.
If someone you know is still missing,
Please personally write me
At JustBeTodd@gmail.com

I will send you a letter letting you know I have placed them on the Official,
Original DRAG Memorial.

I have been your OFFICIAL INTERNATIONAL DRAG HISTORIAN since 2007 with a long proven record to display sincerity. I am not a fan of the term "drag" as applied across this entire art form, but until they find a single word "more accepting," I will have to use it. The drag community has helped me earn twenty LGBT world records. I created DRAG411 to document this form of entertainment. We are the world's largest organization for male, female, and androgynous impersonators with over 7,000 current or former impersonators in 32 countries.

In Memoriam

Wall Postings on DRAG411.com
Updated: 08.02.18 at 10:56 pm (MDT)
1366 names.

Aalbert Martijn Smit,
Aami Dyshea,
Aarica Mincey,
Aarica Shane,
Aaron Von Baron,
Abbey Rhoades,
Aboyda Stragg,
Ada Buffet,
Adam Richards,
Adam West,
Adam Winsor,
Adeva Blaze,
Adoni Bolhar,
Adrain (Ada) James,
Adrain Perez,
Adrella,
Adrian Adair,
Adrian Ames,
Adrian James Thorpe,
Adrian Ty'lle,
Adrienne Ashe,
Africa Brooks,
AJ "Mandi" Millan,
Alan Sheenan,
Alana Kela,
Alanis Laurell,

Alejandro Santana Tavio,
Alex C. (Chucky) Montgomery,
Alex Forrest,
Alex Soto,
Alexandria Diaz,
Alexis Arquette,
Alexis Bone't,
Alexis De'Milo,
Alexis Fairchild,
Alexus,
Alice Kooki H. Mizuki,
Alina Hemingway,
Alisha Harris,
Allan Jarrett,
Allan Maloney,
Alotta Whoremones,
Alyssa Day,
Amancio Corrales,
Amanda Love,
Amanda of the Freak,
Amazing Grace,
Amber Clare,
Amber Haze,
Amber Richards
Amber Richards,
Amber Starr,
Amii Dyshea,
Anastacia Lee,
Andre Adore,
Andre Hale,
Andrea Nicole,
Andy Holmes,
Andy Klitty,
Andy Lucas,
Angel Chico,
Angela Aaron Winchester,
Angela Evans,
Angelica Hines,
Angie DeMarco,
Angie Dickinson,
Angie Xtravaganza,
Anika Glam Moore,
Anita Thomas,
Anthony Jerome Lee,
Anthony Lee,
Anthony Luis Laureano Disla,
Antoine Ashley,
April Eudy Simelane,
April Greer,
Arabia Knight-Addams,
Areatha Flowers,
Aric Potter,
Ariel Andrews,
Ariel Maranda Gibbs

Arthur Caesars,
Arturo Galster,
Ash Barber,
Ashley Adams,
Ashley Alexander,
Ashley Ann Summers,
Ashley Chambers,
Ashley Dior,
Ashley Kelly,
Ashley Kruiz,
Ashley Monroe,
Ashley Nason,
Ashley Paige,
Ashley Summers,
Asia Alexander,
Aspen Love,
Asya Alexander,
Audrey Morgan,
Auntie Flo,
Aunye Iman Diamond,
Avis Pendavis
Avonte Iman,
Barbette,
Barbie Grant,
Barrie Stevens,
Barry Guarino,
Barry Lane Hickey,
Basia,
Bati Star,
Beki Goldstein,
Belle Kinkade,
Benjamin Smoke,
Bernard Alan Davidson,
BernieMacDonald,
Bert Savoy,
Bertha Butts,
Beryl Gumm,
Bette Davis,
Beulah Lemont,
Beverly LaSalle,
Bianca Brinski,
Bianca Davenport Starr,
Bianca DeMonet,
Bianca Paige,
Big Mama,
Big Momma Maybelle,
Bill Roy,
Billie Boots,
Billie Dodson,
Billy "Mother" Boots,
Billy Piper,
Bliss Blaisedale,
Blossom O'Toole,
Bob Gale,

Bobbie Callicoate,
Bobbie Holiday,
Bobbie Janson,
Bobby Compian,
Bobby Crane,
Bobby DeCastro,
Bobby Etienne,
Bobby Marchan,
Bobo O'Neal,
Boi George,
Boom Boom LaTour,
Bothwell Browne,
Brad Hall,
Brandi Houston,
Brandi McDaniels,
Brandy Alexander,
Brandy Dover,
Brazon,
Brenda Blake,
Brenda Dale Knox,
Brenda Lee,
Breneisha,
Brent Moreland,
Bri Alexander,
Brian Benton,
Brian Clark,
Brian Fox,
Brianna Colby,
Britany Fairchild,
British Sterling,
Brittney Wells,
Bruce Falls,
Bruce Williams,
Buffy Demaro,
Buhlah LaMonte,
Bunny Lane,
Bunny Lewis,
Burmon King,
Busty Ross,
Butchie Tanner,
Byron Coleman,
Cameron B. Tanner,
Candi Cabrini,
Candi Wilson,
Candice Carrington,
Candice Kelly,
Candie Van Cartier,
Candy Booth,
Candy Du Barry,
Candy Dubarry,
Candy Wills duBarry,
Cari Wayne,
Carl Rizzi,
Carlotta,

Carmel Santiago,
Carmen Del Rio,
Carmen Rupe,
Carmen,
Carole Jackson,
Carolyn Frye,
Carrie Dennis,
Carrie Phillips,
Casey Cole,
Cashetta,
Cassandra Blake,
Cassandra Gay,
Cassandra Mills-Best,
Catrina Avilon,
CC Lines,
Cece Deval,
CeCe LaCroix
Cedric Patton
Celine Crawford,
Champagne Howell,
Champale Denise,
Chanaile Solitaire,
Chanel Devine Sherrington,
Chanel St. James,
Chanel White,
Chante Seville,
Chantel McKee,
Chantelle Douglas,
Charlene Rose,
Charles Aaron Grimes Winchester,
Charles Ludlam,
Charles McDuff Gillis,
Charles Parr,
Charles Pierce,
Charlie Brown,
Charlie Davis,
Charlotte Parr,
Charlotte,
Chelsea Shanese,
Chena Kelly,
Cherelle Ventura,
Cherine Alexander,
Cherry Cola,
Chi Chi Laverne,
China Doll,
Chip Thomas,
Chivonne Street
Chloe Coleman,
Chocolate Monague,
Chocolate Thunderpussy,
Chris Ames,
Chris Culligan,
Chris Edwards,
Chrissie,

Christi Cole,
Christian Paige,
Christie Cole,
Christie Lane,
Chuck Atteberry,,
Chyna Doll Dupree,
Chyna Gibson,
Ciji Michaels
Cinnamon,
Cissy Goldberg,
Cladette Knight,
Claire Sheradin,
Clarissa Cavalier,
Claudio G. Lake,
Clay Edwin Lambert,
Clay Hester,
Clayton Hamilton,
Clifford Vicks,
Cloe Coleman,
Coco,
Codie Leone,
Codie Ravioli,
Cody McGuire,
Cole Walker,
Colin Devereaux,
Coma,
Connell Howell,
Connie Carlylse,
Connie Dupree,
Connie Marcell,
Constance Calcutta,
Constance Monroe,
Cookie Dough,
Cookie LaCook,
Cookie McCoo Childress,
Corwin Anthony Hawkins,
Cory Good,
Cote' Rossmore,
Craig Loucks,
Craig R. Eadie,
Craig Russell,
Crave Moorehead,
Cruella Divine,
Crystal Clear,
Crystal DeVille,
Crystal Starr,
Crystal,
Daddy K,
Daisy Dalton
Daisy Dube,
Daisy Dynamite,
Dale Johnson,
Dalila,
Dame Glenda,

Dame Hilda Bracket,
Dan Bisson,
Dan Curry,
Danee Russo Rodriquez,
Dani Daletto,
Daniel Booth,
Daniel Crystal,
Daniel D. Perry,
Daniel Davis,
Daniel Patrick Carroll,
Danny Billington,
Danny Day,
Danny Hurshman,
Danny King,
Danny LaRue,
Danny Leonard,
Danny Windsor,
Dante Brown,
Danyelle Winters,
Daphne Delight,
Daphne Devore,
Daphne Prideaux,
Darin Shane Honeycutt,
Darla Childs,
Darla Delicious,
Darren West,
Dave Pollard,
David Cain,
David Desire,
David Feldstein,
David John Wayne MacDonald,
Davina Delmar,
Deborah Debt,
Dede Divore,
Dee Dee Williams,
Deja Knight
Deliah O'Neal,
Della Reeves,
Demetrios "Jimmy" Karahalios,
Dena Malloy,
Dena Michaels,
Denise Darshell,
Denise Fairchild
Denise Michaels,
Dennis VanBelle,
Derek Hood,
DeShawna Hughes,
Desiree Love,
Destiny Foster,
Destiny Rae
Deva Sanchez,
Devine,
Diamond Lil,
Diamonds Lamour,

Diana Black,
Diana Hutton,
Diana Stryker,
Diane Jackson,
Diane Torr,
Dianna Hubbard,
Dick Peltz,
Didi Jagger,
Didi Piaf,
Dion (Martel) Martell,
Dior Dandridge,
Dirt Woman,
Divine,
Dixie Crystals,
Dixie D. Cupp,
Dockyard Doris,
Dolly Love,
Dominique Sanchez,
Don Middlemiss,
Don Seymour McLean,
Donald E. Smith,
Donald George Shelton,
Donald W. Davis,
Donna Day,
Donna Drag,
Donni DuPont,
Donnie Corker,
Dorian Corey
Dorian Wayne,
Doris Fish,
Dottie West,
Doug Austen,
Dougie Anderson,
Dreama Andrews,
Drew Mancuso,
Duncan Do Not,
Dusti Hymen,
Dusty Deville,
Dusty Diamond,
Dyan Michaels,
Dyanna Stryker,
Dyiamond Dynasty,
Ebony Hall,
Ebony,
Ed Wood,
Eddie Bell,
Edie Holiday,
Edward Davis "Ed" Wood Jr.,
Edye Goldsby, aka
Edye Gregory,
Elaine St. Jaques,
Ellen Diamond,
Endora Van Cartier Clinton,
Enrique Hinojosa Vázquez,

Epiphanie,
Eric Farrow,
Erica Adams,
Erica Andrews,
Erica Lane,
Erica Lucci,
Erica Meadows,
Erica Renee Knight,
Erica Shane,
Erica Sommers,
Erica Van Cort,
Erik Johnston,
Erik Knight,
Erika Mills,
Esteban Romero,
Ethel Bailey,
Ethyl Eichelberger,
Eva Destruction,
Evan St. John,
Eve Starr,
Evelyn Davis,
Evelyn Sanchez,
Fabiola,
Faith Iman,
Farrah Amanda McCray,
Felicia Adams,
Felicia Gallant,
Felicia Mark,
Felicia Mortuiccio,
Felicia Winters,
Felitia Fahr,
Felton Day,
Feral Beral,
Fernando Gomez,
Flawless Sabrina,
Flo Floé,
Fonda C. Lord,
Foo Foo (Lamarr) Lammar
Fran Jeffries,
Francis Leon,
Francis Patrick Glassey,
Francis Renault,
Francis Russell,
Frank Adair,
Frank Devera Jackson,
Frank Doran,
Frank Lamarr,
Frank Pearson,
Frankie Barry,
Frankie Jaxon,
Fred Cougan,
Freddy Renault,
Fritz Capone,
Gabrielle "Gabby" Berlyn,

Gabrielle Sizemore,
Garfield West,
Gary Gagnon,
Gary Mangum,
Gary McMurtry,
Gayla Mccord Delust,
Gayle Lynn,
Gemini,
Gene La Marr,
Gene Malin,
George Peduzzi,
Georgia Brown,
Gerard George Andrews,
Geri Day,
Gib Hauersperger,
Gigi,
Gilbert Baker,
Gina De Anton,
Ginger Lamar,
Ginger Nichole,
Ginger Spice,
Ginger Taylor,
Ginger Vitus,
Gita Gilmore,
Glam Moore,
Glen Paulin,
GlenGlen Wagner,
Grand Prix,
Grande,
Great Scagnolia,
Gregory Cohn,
Gregory Courtesis,
Guilda,
Guy Carroll,
Hal Wadell,
Hank Lintjer,
Hans van den Hoek,
Harold Waller,
Harris Glenn Milstead,
Harry S. Franklyn,
Harvey Lee,
Heather Anton,
Heather D'Haven,
Heather Hunter,
Heavy Metal,
Henry Boyd,
Hillary Matthews,
Hollie Wood,
Holly Brown,
Holly Daze Crystals,
Holly St. Clair,
Holly Woodlawn,
Hope Holloway,
Howard Meyer,

Howard Shortsleeve,
Howard Tipler,
Hunter Smith,
Ignacio Rodriguez,
Image Devereux,
Imani Tate,
Imogene Wilson,
Indigo Luvsumme Blue,
Irving Ale,
Isabella Frost,
Issan Dorsey,
Issy St. James Escada,
Ivana / Ivanna,
Ivonna Hump,
Ivory Díor,
Ivy White,
Jack Doroshow,
Jack Roberts,
Jackie Roberts,
Jackie Wilson,
Jacqueline Pissybottom
Jae Stevens,
Jagger Blue,
Jahnau Reis,
Jalissa Aundrea Michaels,
James Arthur Fuller,
James Carroll,
James Clark,
James Crews,
James Harrington,
James Levi,
James McDowell,
James Pascoe,
James Roy Eichelberger,
James St. James,
James Thorpe,
Jamie Carroll,
Jamie Christian,
Jamie Levi,
Jamie Silver,
Jan Chamblee,
Jan Howard,
Jan Payne,
Jana Steele,
Jarmon Mayes,
Jasmine Knight,
Jasmine Perry,
Jason Bradley,
Jason Lincoln,
Jason-Ivy White,
Javon Phelps,
Jay Monro,
Jay Russel,
Jayda Beyonce Taylor,

Jazz,
Jean Guida de Mortellaro,
Jean Malin,
Jeanetta Williams
Jeanie "Tits" Duval,
Jeff Gibson,
Jeff Tagg,
Jeffrey Lithcum,
Jemma Storm,
Jennifer Harlow,
Jennifer Lakes,
Jennifer North,
Jennifer Raquel,
Jennifer Welles,
Jenny McCall,
Jere Williams,
Jerri Daye,
Jerry Clanton,
Jerry Luna-Rockwell,
Jesse Scott,
Jessenia Marie Rosa,
Jessica Jackson,
Jessica Jazz Ross,
Jessica Nolan,
Jill Jordan,
Jill-Ette Knicks,
Jim Bailey,
Jim Peterson,
Jimi Dee,
Jimmie Dee,
Jimmy Clem,
Jimmy Dillard,
Jimmy McCollough,
Jimmy Smith,
JoAnn Delite,
Jocelyn Anthony,
Joe Cline,
Joe Collins,
Joe Jackson,
Joel Castillo,
Johanna Steel,
John Anthony Gonzales,
John Atkinson,
John Barber,
John Byrne,
John Cely,
John Gonzales,
John Harvey,
John Lonas,
John Martin,
John Palmer,
John Schaefe,
John Zarrelli,
Johnelle Vincent,

Johnny Maddox,
JoJo,
Jolie London,
Jordan Alexander,
Jordan Blake
José Julio Sarria,
Joseph Stevens,
Josh Hamburg,
Joshua Horton,
Josie Desmond,
Judy Judy,
Julian Eltinge,
Junior Larkin,
K.C. Carrington,
Kaitlyn Cain
Kandy Johnson,
Kara Dion,
Karl Williams,
Karlita,
Karyl Norman,
Katrina Avalon,
Katrina Gail Phillips,
Kay Mullinax,
Kelley,
Kelly Dagen
Kelly King,
Kelly Summers,
Kelvin Bradley Watkins,
Kendra Monroe,
Kenneth Melo,
Kenneth Poole,
Kenny Dash,
Kenny Kerr,
Kenny Leda,
Kenny Whitehead,
Keosha Necole "Keke"Cassadine,
Kerri O'Kee,
Ketty Teanga,
Kevin Bauer,
Kevin Dorsey,
Kevin Rodriquez,
Kevin Vaughan,
Kiarra Cartier Fontaine,
KiArra Fontaine Marlowe,
Kiarra St. James,
Kiki DeCarlo,
Kiki,
Kiki, Mother,
Kim Alexis,
Kim Ross,
Kim Valdez,
Kim, Connors,
Kimberly "KJ" Morris,
Kirby Kincade,

Kitten Do Claw,
Kitty Collins,
Kitty DeLove,
Kitty Litter,
Klitty Liqour,
Kolby Kincaid,
Kristina Grant Infiniti,
Kristina Grant,
Kristy Love,
Krystal Kelly,
Krystal Stone,
Kylie O'Reilly
La Twig Darling,
Lady Ashley Adams,
Lady Barbara,
Lady Baroness Maria Andrea del Santiago,
Lady Cateria,
Lady Catira,
Lady Chablis,
Lady Charles,
Lady Charlotte,
Lady D,
Lady Diana,
Lady Ebony Hall,
Lady Gayle,
Lady Geneva,
Lady Godiva,
Lady Helena Sacowitz,
Lady Katiria,
Lady Nova Bernard,
Lady Pearl,
Lady Shawn,
Lady Vic,
Lady Wincey,
Lana Kuntz,
Larista Colby,
Larry Fox,
Larry Huggins,
Larry Kidd,
Larry Love,
Lateasha Shante Shuntel,
Latese Chevron,
LaTorsha Zannel,
Latoya St. James
Laura Beth,
Laura Lee Love,
Lauren LaMasters,
Lauren Sugarbaker,
Lauryn Paige Fuller,
LaVern Banadese
Laverne Cummings,
Laviita Allen,
Lee Paris,
Lee Stevens,

Leif Roschberg,
Leigh Bowery,
Lena London,
Lennie LaToke,
Leonard Kelly,
Leonardo Martinez,
Leslie Rage,
Leslie Rajanne,
Leslie Woods,
Lester Childress,
Lestra La Monte,
Letha Weapons,
Lexie Love,
Lilian Carré,
Linda Day,
Linda Robinson,
Lindsey Love,
Liquor Campbell,
Lisa Fontaine,
Lisa King,
Logan Carter,
Lona LaMore
Lonnie McElwain,
Lori Shannon,
Lotta Nerve,
Lulu LaRude,
Lupi Longoria,
Luther Nelson Jr.,
Lyndell Honeycutt,
Maddox Madison,
Mag Reiley,
Maggie London,
Maggie Scott,
Magnolia Thunderpussy,
Mahogany Reason,
Mahogany,
Malcom Michaels Jr.,
Malissa Starr,
Mallessa Starr,
Mama,
Mame Dennis,
Manzell Avant,
Marc Beuter,
Marc Fleming,
Marcy Marcell,
Margo Howard-Howard,
Margo,
Maria Mendez,
Marilyn Chambers,
Mario Bermudez,
Mark Fleming,
Mark Irish,
Mark Middleton,
Mark William Irish,

Marnie,
Mars,
Marsha P. Johnson,
Marty McClain,
Mary Kaye,
Marylin Lee,
Matthew Bogseth,
Matthew Burk,
Maurice Carter,
Maxi Houston,
Maxine Allen,
Maxwell Ritchie,
Maya M. Moore,
Melba Moore,
Melissa D'Moore,
Mellisa Blake,
Melvin Leachman,
Memory Lane,
Memphis Deville Richards,
Mercedes Demarco,
Mercedes Gallant,
Mercedes Successful,
Merlin D "Tommy" Thompson,
Merph/Murph Griffin,
Meshallay Crystal,
Mia Landon,
Michael Andrews,
Michael Androlewicz,
Michael Canterbury,
Michael Clarke,
Michael Leonard Williams, KSG,
Michael Murphy,
Michael Skaggs,
Michael St Laurent,
Michelle Christina Jones,
Michelle Le'More,
Michelle Liemont,
Michelle Marie,
Michelle Scott
Michelle St James,
Michelle St. John,
Mickey Day,
Mickey LaRue,
Mickie Knight,
Midnight Annie,
Mike Cain,
Milla,
Milton Berle,
Mishon Black,
Miss Chifon,
Miss DeJa Vous
Miss Demeanor,
Miss Ebony,
Miss Kitty,

Miss Mann,
Miss Marcus,
Miss Markus,
Miss Opal Foxx,
Miss Opal,
Miss P.,
Miss Petra Fyde,
Miss Tracy,
Miss Understood.
Miss Vogue,
Miss Woochie,
Miss-ter Billie Pet Clarke,
Misty Knight,
Misty McCall,
Mitch Bartlett,
Mizz Ginger,
Moldavia Ishtar,
Molly Redmond,
Mona Desmond,
Mona Leather,
Monica Marlo,
Monica Rey,
Monique Moore,
Morgan Courday,
Morgan Courtnay Deveraux,
Morgan Farrah,
Morgan St. Clair,
Morgan Wood,
Morrie Carter,
Morticia DeVille,
Mother Detroit,
Mr. Bunny Lewis,
Mr. Chip Thomas,
Mr. Crystal,
Mr. Della Reeves,
Mr. Sandy Howard,
Mr. Terry Durham,
Mr. Tiffany Jones,
Mrs. Shufflewick,
Ms. Dee,
Ms. Marcus,
Mya Mokka Iman,
Myla Larue,
Myrna Vonn,
Naiomy Kane,
Naomi Sims,
Natalie Gaye LaShore,
Natalie Greer,
Natasha Edwards,
Natasha Fields,
Natasha Hall,
Natasha Richards,
Neal Horvatits,
Neal O'Hara,

Neal Scott,
Neely O'Hara,
Netasha Edwards,
Nia Gabrielle,
Nichelle Nichols,
Nick Connor,
Nicki Gallucci,
Nicky Young,
Nikki Fenmore,
Nikki LeParks,
Nikki Silvers,
Nikki Starr,
Nikki Young Blackpool,
Nina Monroe,
Nina Rage,
Noel Dougherty,
Nomi De'Vereaux,
Norris Benefield
Obvious Heights,
Octavia St. Laurent,
Odyssey
Olivia Pantene,
Opal Fox,
Owen Pride Roach,
Paal Roschberg,
Paddy Kakes,
Paivi Lee Love,
Paris Chanel,
Paris Dupree
Patricia Murphy,
Patrick Callahan,
Patrick Fyffe,
Patrick McGuire,
Patrick Murphy,
Patrina Marie,
Patsy Vidalia,
Patti Cakes,
Patty Kakes,
Paul Ashford,
Paulettea Leigh,
Pauline St. James,
Peach Melba,
Peaches LaFleur,
Peg A Go-Go,
Peg,
Penelope Poupé,
Penelope,
Pepper LaBeija,
Peter Fernandez,
Peter Searle,
Petrina Marie,
Phil Starr,
Philip Mills,
Phillip Forrester,

Phillip Rhoads,
Poison,
Porscha Mercadez,
Prdra Austell Hall,
Prince D Andrews,
Princess Janae Banks,
Prissy Divine,
Prudence,
Pussy Willow,
Quinton Crisp,
R.C. Cola,
R.V. Beaumont,
Rachael Leigh,
Rachael Masters,
Rachaell Santoni,
Rachel Winters,
Racine Scott,
Rae Bourbon,
Raine Scott,
Ramona Baker,
Ramona LeGer,
Ramona Ravenski,
Randy Cole,
Ray Francis,
Raymond Fetcho,
RD Walls,
Reg Bundy,
Regina Fong,
Reginald Sutherland Bundy,
Reina Valentino,
Rene Russo,
Rene Van Hulle,
Renée Scott,
Renee Williams,
Reuben Bressler,
Reviala Donroe,
Rex Jameson,
Rhonda Leigh,
Rhonda Moore,
Rhonda Starr,
Ric DiMario,
Ricci Russeaux,
Richard Greer,
Richard Hall,
Richard Henson,
Richard Hoffman,
Richard Masterson,
Richard Nichols,
Richard Palsgrove,
Richard Reese,
Richard Thomas,
Richard Webb,
Ricky Carter,
Ricky Cordova,

Ricky Glass,
Ricky Renee,
Rikki Lee,
Roada Kihl,
Robbie Walker,
Robert Booth,
Robert Hesse,
Robert Logan Carter,
Robert Mitchel-Blough,
Robert Penninger,
Robert Robinson,
Robert Timbrell,
Robert Wanke,
Robin Banks,
Robin Wayne,
Robyn Hunter,
Roger Godfrey,
Romona Lager,
Ronald Davis,
Ronald Dennison,
Ronald Jerome Alford,
Rondretta Billingsly,
Ronica Reed,
Ronnie McDaniel,
Ronnie Reed,
Rosa Lake,
Rosalyn Delight,
Rose Leaf,
Rose Marie,
Rose Petal,
Roshawn Greer,
Rosheda Tyia,
Rosie Marie,
Roski Fernandez,
Roslyn Heights,
Ross Higham,
Roxanne Cordova,
Roxanne O'Neil,
Roxanne Russell,
Roxanne,
Roxie Cotton,
Roy L Derryberry,
Roy Steel,
Royal Knight,
Ruby Dee,
Ruby Flame,
Rudi D'Angelo,
Rudi Rogelio,
Rudy de La Mor,
Rudy L. Hendrickson,
Russell Craig Eadie,
Rusty Ryan,
Ruud Swanen,
RV Beaumont,

Ryan Zinc,
Ryk McDow,
Sabel D' Zyre,
Sable Starr,
Sabre Patton,
Sabrina Morgan,
Sache VanCartier,
Sadie Brooks,
Safari Habiel,
Sahara Davenport,
Sally Mae Sasquatch,
Samantha Cleavage,
Samantha Love,
Samantha,
Sammy Duddy,
Sammy Thomas,
Samuel Collins,
Sandee,
Sandi Lovelace,
Sandra Hush,
Sandra Hush,
Sandra Playgirl,
Sandy Cher,
Sandy Howard,
Sandy K. Daniels,
Santana T. Summers,
Sasha Kennedy,
Sasha Loren,
Sasha Nicole,
Sasha Valentino,
Sassie Saltimboca,
Satan Deville,
Satara Shatin,
Satin Rose,
Satin Styles,
Satryana Blaque,
Satyn DeVille,
Savannah Kohl
Savion Simpson Black,
Savona Campbell,
Scabola,
Scarlett Fever,
Scott Andrew,
Scott Weston,
Selena Daniels,
Sensuous,
Serena Hunter,
Shafonda Vaughn,
Shahgopal Whybrow,
Shakira Stevenz,
Shan Covington,
Shana Steele,
Shanell Solitaire,
Shangay Lily,

Shanice Starr,
Shannon Forrester,
Shavon Marlon Shawn,
Shayla Masters,
Shayla Simpson,
Sheena Angelica,
Sheila T. Bailey,
Shelita Golden,
Shelly Stout,
Sheree Franklin,
Shereen Dennis,
Sheri Powers,
Shirleena,
Shirley Steel,
Shirley Wood,
Shirley,
Sicely Manchester,
Sidney Headburg,
Sierra Montana,
Sinclair,
Sissy Collins,
Sister Roma,
Skip Arnold,
Sofonda L. Peters,
South Beach Wanda,
Sovereign Rey'al,
Stacey Brown,
Stacey Lauren
Stacia Leron,
Stacy Farrare,
Starr LaSalle,
Stasha Iman,
Stazia,
Stella Show Icmeler,
Steph Sparkles,
Stephani Stamos,
Stephanie Bofill,
Stephanie Powers,
Stephany "Sticky" Daniels,
Stephen Cann,
Stephen L. Jones,
Steve Boeger,
Steve Jones,
Steven Dale Renner,
Steven Gelley,
Steven Magyarics,
Steven Michael Egan,
Steven Nelson,
Steven Teets,
Steven Yablonski,
Stevie Stevens,
Stormé DeLarverie
Strawbella Be'AGoddess,
Studio X Lenoir,

Sultanna Corangie,
Summer Holiday,
Summer Holliday,
Sweetie,
Sybil Ann Storm, aka
Sybil Santiago,
Sybil Smith
Sylvester James, Jr.,
Sylvester,
Synoman,
T. C. Jones,
Tabitha Stevens,
Tabitha Versace Starr,
Tahtiana Kresha,
Tajma Hall,
Tallulah Banks,
Tallulah,
Tam Taylor,
Tamara Demore,
Tamara Fox,
Tami DeLove,
Tammy Pax,
Tandi Andrews,
Tandi Dupree,
Tandi Iman Dupree,
Tanisha Cassadine,
Tanisha Caston,
Tara Dion,
Tara Richmond,
Tara Schenelle Starr,
Tara-Ash Barber,
Tasha Diane,
Tatiannah Kreshe,
Taylor Hill,
Teddy Pedigree Paul,
Teighlor Artesk,
Temple,
Teri Courtney,
Teri Jean Arnell,
Terri Livingston,
Terri Michaels,
Terri Rodgers,
Terri Rogers,
Terri-Jean Arnell,
Terry Cummings,
Terry Durham,
Terry Gardner,
Terry Jean Arnell,
Terry Knight,
Terry La Tour,
Terry Livingston,
Terry Matthews,,
Terry Parnell,
Terry Phillips,

TeTe Torez,
The Diva Perry,
The Lady Chablis,
The Tigress,
The Widow Norton,
Thomas Craig "T. C." Jones,
Thomas Fairmakes,
Thomas Lincon,
Tifani St Jon,
Tiffani Jones,
Tiffany Daniels,
Tiffany Jones,
Tiffany Rose,
Tiffany Scott,
Tiger Lil',
Tillie Plumkin,
Tim Gillan,
Tim Greeley,
Tim Moore,
Timi Tremaine,
Timothy Liupakka,
Timothy Swain,
Tina Braxton,
Tina Renee,
Tina Roberts,
Tina Schumacher,
Tina Templeton,
Tina Wells,
Tiny Tina,
Tippi Walker
Tippy Hedron,
Tippy,
Tish Tanner,
Tissy Malone,
Toby Marsh,
Todd Estes,
Todd Shelf,
Todd Storti,
Tom Yaegy,
Tommy Dee,
Tommy Dorsey, Jr.,
Tommy McGuire,
Toni Duran,
Toni Lenoir,
Toni Lenore,
Tony Bua,
Tony Rose,
Tony Sinclair,
Tonya Gayle,
Tonya Mullins,
Torchie Taylor,
Torchy Lane,
Torrance Cheeves,
Torre Adore,

Totie Martel,
Trace McNutt,
Tracey Lee,
Tracey Nichols,
Tracey Stephens,
Tracey Stephens,
Tracey Stevens
Tracy "Liz" Adams,
Tracy Adams,
Tracy Fontain,
Tracy Morgan,
Tracy Savage,
Tranny Robert,
Trauma Flintstone,
Travis Gore,
Travis Mark Michael Greenfield,
Treasure Gardener,
Treva Perry,
Trevor Rupe,
Tricksie Turner,
Trinity Scott Mathews,
Trisha Trash,
Trixie Daily,
Trixie Taylor,
Troy James "Dusty" Lansdown,
Troy Williams,
Truley LeFemme,
Truman May,
TT Thompson,
Tu Real,
Tuna Starr
Tuna Starr,
Tweeka Weed,
Twiggy,
Tyler Wicihowski,
Tyra Bishop,
Valencia Rollins,
Vander Clyde,
Vanessa Dell Rio,
Vanessa LaSalle,
Vanessa Michelle,
Vanessa Richards,
Vanessa Vanover Vermont,
Vanilla Lush,
Vanity Munroe,
Vanity Starr,
Vaunda Lee,
Vaunessa Vale,
Venus Xtravaganza,
Veronica Devore,
Veronica Grey,
Veronica Lake,
Veronica York,
Vicci Laine,

Vicki Lawrence,
Vicki Marlane,
Vicki Martin,
Vicki Rene,
Vickii Vox,
Vicky Mandrell,
Victor Guimarães,
Victoria Burton,
Victoria Lamarr,
Victoria Sinclair,
Victoria St. James,
Victoria Towers,
Vidas de Herejes,
Vincent Hill,
Vinny Lick Her Snatch,
Vivienne Fontana St. James,
Vonda Delaine,
Vonda Lee,
Vonda Richards,
Vonna Valentino,
Walter Bell,
Walter Dempster, Jr.
Walter Flemming,
Walter Hart,
Walterina Markova,
Wanda Lust,
Warren Wilson,
Waylon Flowers,
Wayne Lee Killough, Jr,
Wayne Smart,
Wesley Aurick McArthur,
Whitney Jackson,
Whitney Paige,
William Albert Castellano,
William Brett Basher,
William Jackson,
William Julian Dalton,
William L Dodson,
Willie Ninja,
Yazmina Couture,
Zena Kay Diamonte,
Zena Kay,
Zsa Zsa D'laHor, and
Zsa Zsa Principle.

Please go to DRAG411.com to see the most updated list
and to ensure no name is missing.

Ten Black Books

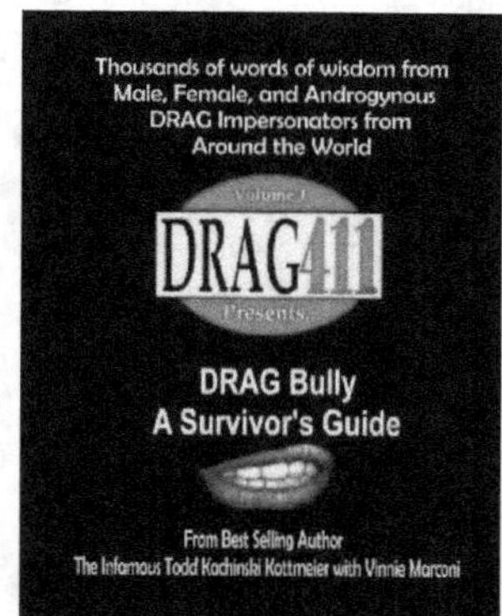

Book 1 DRAG411's
"DRAG Bully, A Survivor's Guide"

The Largest Bullying Project in LGBT History for Struggling Entertainers. Advice from over a hundred male, female, and androgynous impersonators around the world to help entertainers struggling with their family, peers, relationships, neighbors, regular jobs, venues, and successfully overcoming self-doubt. Best Selling author Todd Kachinski Kottmeier created DRAG411 to document the lives of male, female, and androgynous impersonator years ago. It is now the largest organization for impersonators on earth with over 7,000 entertainers in 32 countries. DRAG411 also operates The International Original, Official DRAG Memorial with almost a thousand names (2018). This is his 25th book, 20th World Record, and 12th book on this subject. Thousands of invitations to contribute were send out. This book contains the best of their responses, in their own words, to you.

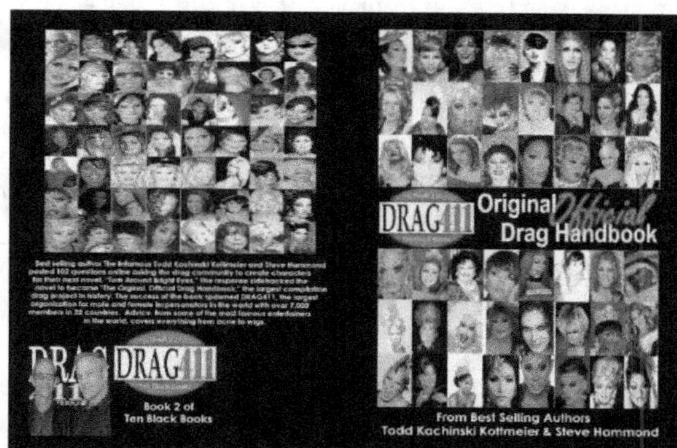

Book 2 DRAG411's
"Original DRAG Handbook"

Over 155 female impersonators (and 1 male impersonator) from around the world share over a thousand insightful comments in the first handbook created of this art form.

Commentary shared with Todd Kachinski Kottmeier included the following contributors of The Original, DRAG Handbook to include Ada Buffet, Adora , Adrian Leigh, Afeelya Bunz, Alisa Summers, Alanna Divine, Alexis De La Mer, Alexis Mateo, Alex Serpa, Allure, Amanda Bone, Amanda Love, Amy DeMilo, Anastaia Fallon, Astasnaia Rexia, Angel gLamar, Angela Dodd, Anita Cox, April Fresh, Ashleigh Cooley, Aurora Sexton, Babette Schwartz, Bailey St. James, Barbra Herr, Barbra Seville, Beverly LaSalle, BJ Stephens, Blair Michaels, Brandon M. Caten, Brianna Lee, Brittany Moore, Brookyln Bisette, Bukkake Blaque London St. James, Cartier Paris, Cathy Craig, Champagne T. Bordeaux, Cherry Darling, Christina Paris, CoCo LaBelle, CoCo Montrese, CoCo St. James, Conundrum, Crystal Belle, Daniel Murphy, Danika Fierce, Daphne Ferraro, Dasha Nicole, Dee Gregory, Deva DaVyne, Diamond Dunhill, Diedra Windsor Walker, Dmentia Divinyl/Eva LaDeva, Echo Dazz, Esme Russell, Estelle Rivers, Eunyce Raye, Felica Fox, Felina Cashmere, Geraldine Queen Cabaret, Ginger Minj, Glitz Glam, Gilda Golden, Horchata, Ima Twat, Ineeda Twat, Jade Daniels, Jade Jolie, Jade Shanell, Jade Sotomayo, Jaeda Fuentes, Jami Micheals, Jay Santana, Jeffrey Powell, Jenna Chambers Tisdale, Jessica Jade, Jocelyn Summers, Jodie Holliday, Joey Brooks, Joshua Myers, J.P. Patrick, Juwanna Jackson, Kamden Wells, Katrina Starr, Kenny Braverman, Khrystal Leight, Kier Sarkesian, Kiki LaFlare Santangilo, Kitty D'Meaner, Kori Stevens, Krystal Amore Adonis, Lacey Lynn Taylors, Lady Clover Honey, Lady Sabrina, Lady TaJma Hall, Lakeisha Pryce, LeeAnna Love, Leigh Shannon, Lisa Carr, Lola Honey, Madisyn De

La Mer, Makayla Rose Devine, Maxine Padlock (Maxi Pad), Melissa Morgan, Melody Mayheim, Michael Wilson, Mike Astermon-Glidden, Mis Sadistic, Miss Conception, Miss Gigi, Mr. Kenneth Blake, Misty Eyez, Monique Michaels, Myah Monroe, Mystique Summers, Nairobi V. D'Viante, Naomi D-Lish, Naomi Wynters, Nicole Paige Brooks, Nikki Dynamite, Nova Starr, Ororo, Patrica Grand, Patricia Knight, Patrica Mason, Pandora DeStrange, Penelope Reigns, Polly FunkChanel, Phiore Star Liemont, Purrzsa Kyttyn, Pussy LeHoot, Raquel Payne, Rhyana Vorhman, Rickie Lee, Rusti Fawcett, Scarlett Fever, Selina Kyle, Shae Shae LaReese, Shealita Babay, Shugah Caine, Stephanie Roberts, Stephanie Stuart, Stormy Vain, Summer Breeze, Sybil Storm, Tabatha Lovall, Tatum Michelle, Teri Courtney, Tiffani Middlesexx, Timm McBride, Toni Davyne, TotiYanah Diamond,Trixie LaRue, Trixie Pleasures, Vegas Platinum, Venus D Lite, Vivika D'Angelo, Wendel Duppert and Wendy G. Kennedy.

Book 3:   DRAG411's
"Crown Me! Winning Pageants"

Hundreds of invitations sent to the titleholders, pageant promoters, judges, and talent show hosts to share their insight on not only winning pageants and contests but also owning the stage every time they perform. Their topics included auxiliary steps to success needed for song selection, dancing, movement on stage, props, backup dancers, creating your own edge, personal interviews, steps to success for winning the talent category every time you step on stage, on stage questions, eveningwear, and creative costuming. They discussed in their own unedited words, wardrobe changes, makeup, hair, shoes, when is the time to compete, qualities needed for a judge, and the top misconceptions of contestants competing in the pageantry systems.

Commentary shared with Todd Kachinski Kottmeier included the following contributors of Crown Me! to include AJ Menendez, Amy Demilo, Anastacia Dupree, Anson Reign, Bob Taylor, Breonna Tenae, Brittany T Moore, Coco Montrese, Dana Douglas, Darryl Kent, Denise Russell, Dey Jzah Opulent, Freddy Prinze Charming, Gage Gatlyn, Jay Santana , Jayden Knight, Jennifer Foxx, Joey Jay, Kori Stevens, Mis Sadistic, Mykul Jay Valentine, Natasha Richards, Rico Taylor, Sam Hare, Stephanie Stuart, Taina T. Norell, Tiffani Middlesexx, Tori Taylor, Ty Nolan, Vinnie Marconi, and Vivika D'Angelo.

Book 4:   DRAG411's
"DRAG King Guide"

Over 155 male impersonators around the world share over a thousand insightful comments in forty-one chapters.

Commentary shared with Todd Kachinski Kottmeier included the following contributors of The Official DRAG King and Male Impersonators Guide to include Aaron Phoenix, Abs Hart, Adam All, Adam DoEve, AJ Menendez, Alec Allnight, Alexander Cameron, Alik Muf, Andrew Citino,   Anjie Swidergal, Anson Reign, Ashton The Adorable Lover, Atown, Ayden Layne, B J Armani, B J Bottoms, Bailey Saint James, Ben Doverr, Ben Eaten, Bootzy Edwards Collynz, Brandon KC Young-Taylor, Bruno Diaz, Cage Masters, Campbell Reid Andrews, Chance Wise, Chandler J Hart, Chasin Love, Cherry Tyler

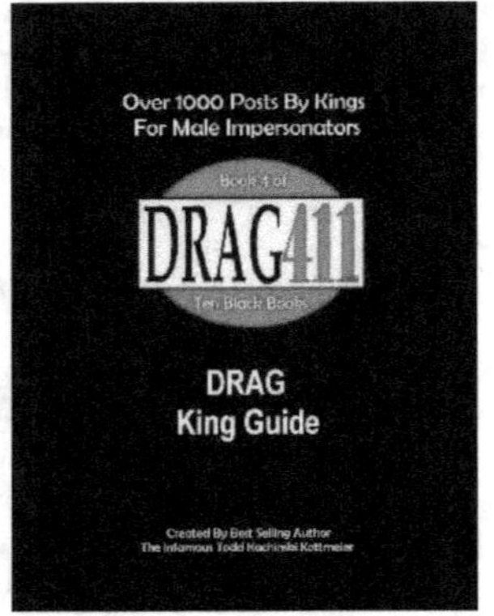

Manhattan, Chris Mandingo, Clark Kunt, Clint Torres, Cody Wellch Klondyke, Colin Grey, Corey James Caster, Coti Blayne, Crash Bandikok, Dakota Rain, Dante Diamond, Davion Summers, DeVery Bess, Devin G. Dame, Devon Ayers, Dionysus W Khaos, Diseal Tanks Roberts, D-Luv

Saviyon, Dominic Demornay, Dominic Von Strap, D-Rex, Dylan Kane, E. M. Shaun, Eddie C. Broadway, Emilio, Erick LaRue, Flex Jonez, Freddy Prinze Charming, Gabe King, Gage Gatlyn, George De Micheal, Greyson Bolt, Gunner Gatlyn, Gus Magendor, Hawk Stuart, Harry Pi, Holden Michael, Howie Feltersnatch, Hurricane Savage, J Breezy St James, Jack E. Dickinson, Jack King, Jake Van Camp, Jamel Knight, Jenson C. Dean, Johnnie Blackheart, Jonah Godfather of DRAG, Jordan Allen, Jordan Reighn, Joshua K. Mann, Joshua Micheals, Juan Kerr, Julius M. SeizeHer, Jude Lawless, Justin Cider, Justin Luvan, Justin Sider, K'ne Cole, Kameo Dupree, Kenneth J. Squires, King Dante, King Ramsey, Jack Inman, Kody Sky, Koomah, Kristian Kyler, Kruz Mhee, Linda Hermann-Chasin, Luke Ateraz, Lyle Love-It, Macximus, Marcus Mayhem, Marty Brown, Master Cameron Eric Leon, Max Hardswell, MaXx Decco, Michael Christian, Mike Oxready, Miles Long, Mr-Charlie Smith, Nanette D'angelo Sylvan, Nolan Neptune, Orion Blaze Browne, Owlejandro Monroe, Papa Cherry, Papi Chulo, Papi Chulo Doll, Persian Prince, Phantom, Pierce Gabriel, Rasta Boi Punany, Rico M Taylor, Rock McGroyn, Rocky Valentino, Rogue DRAG King, Romeo Sanchez, Rychard "Alpha" Le'Sabre, Ryder Knightly, Ryder Long, Sam Masterson, Sammy Silver, Santana Romero, Scorpio, Shane Rebel Caine, Shook ByNature, Silk Steele Prince, SirMandingo Thatis, Smitty O'Toole, Soco Dupree, Spacee Kadett, Starr Masters, Stefan LeDude, Stefon Royce Iman, Stefon SanDiego, Stormm, Teddy Michael, Thug Passion, Travis Luvermore, Travis Hard, Trey C. Michaels, Trigger Montgomery, Tyler Manhattan, Viciouse Slick, Vinnie Marconi, Welland Dowd, William Vanity Matrix, Wulf Von Monroe, Xander Havoc, and Xavier Bottoms.

Book 5:   DRAG411's
"DRAG Stories"

Funny stories shared with Todd Kachinski Kottmeier including the following contributors of DRAG Stories to include Chance Wise, Anson Reign, Tiffani Middlesexx, Rico Taylor, Todd Kachinski Kottmeier, Bob Taylor, Stefon Royce Iman, Candi Samples, Alexis Mateo, Naomi Wynters, Dmentia Divinyl, Bruce Lacie, Kennedy Wendy, Chastity Rose, Miss GiGi, Angel gLamar, Patricia Grand, Shook ByNature, Lady Guy, Eunyce Raye, Charley Marie Coutora, Jezzie Bell, Lamar Kellam, Jayden St. James, Rachelle Ann Summers, Champagne T Bordeaux, Gilda Golden, Daisha Monet, Vivika D'Angelo, Rachel Boheme, Esme Rodriguez, and MaNu Da Original.

Book 6:   DRAG411's
"DRAG Mother, DRAG Father" Honoring Mentors

Performers look to DRAG mothers, DRAG fathers, friends, and fans for insight, compassion, and guidance as mentors. This book honors those special people. Over 140 entertainers contributed wisdom and words for this historical book, making it the largest project of its nature in GLBTQ history and the first published book on male and female mentors.

Commentary shared with Todd Kachinski Kottmeier included the following contributors of DRAG Parents to includee AJ Menendez, Vinnie Marconi, Mis Sadistic, Todd Kachinski Kottmeier, Bob Taylor, Taina Norell, Andrew Stratton, Horchata Horchata, David Warner, Gianna Love, Trinity Taylor, Domunique Jazmin Vizcaya, Brittany Moore, PurrZsa Kyttyn, Jake Lickus, Shelita Taylor, Adriana Manchez, MiMi Welch, China Taylor, Armondis Bone't, Monique Trudeau, Simeon Codfish, Diamond Dupree, Stefon Royce Iman, Jayden Stjames, Demonica da Bomb, Colin Grey, Christopher Todd Guy, Celyndra Lashay Clyne, Candice St. James, Justin Barnes Williams, Ivanna Dooche, London Taylor Douglas, Christina Alexandria Victoria Regina Lowe, Bianca DeMonet, Critiqa Mann, Jazmen Andrews, AJ Allen, TotiYanah Diamond, D' Marco Knight, Chip Matthews, Mirage Montrese, India Starr Simms, Jade S Stratton, Emerald Divine, Elysse Giovanni, Vanity Halston, Kristofer Reynolds, Akasha Uravitch, Adriana Fuentes, Erykah Mirage, Felicity Ferraro, Joey Payge, Rhiannon Todd, Vicious Slick, Amirage Saling, Tori Sass, Chy'enne Valentino, and Robbi Lynn.

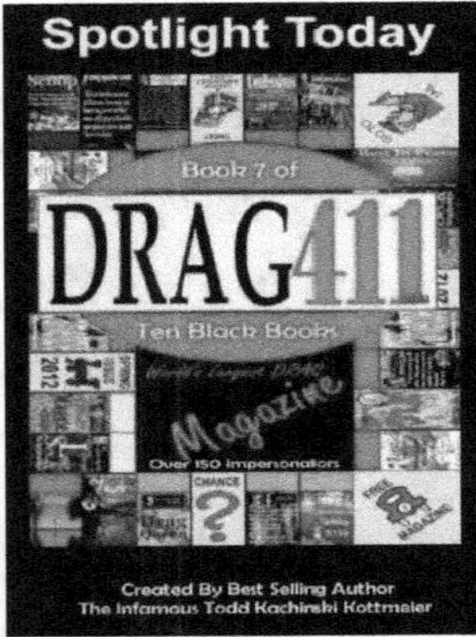

Book 7: DRAG411's
"Spotlight Today"

It was the World's Largest Paperback Magazine for Impersonators and Fans when it premiered with over 175 pages. DRAG411 no longer prints Spotlight Today Magazine, but here is the re-release of the groundbreaking first edition. Complete articles by Vinnie Marconi, Denise Russell, Tiffani T. Middlesexx, Kristofer Reynolds, Magenta Alexandria Dupree, Butch Daddy, Vivikah Kayson-Raye, Makanoe, Amanda Lay, Thomas DeVoyd, Kevin B. Reed, Glenn Storm, and over 150 impersonators from around the world.

Book 8:   DRAG411's
"DRAG Queen Guide"

Almost two hundred female impersonators around the world share over a thousand insightful comments in forty-one chapters.

Commentary shared with Todd Kachinski Kottmeier included the following contributors of Official DRAG Queen and Female Impersonator Handbook to include Alana Summers, Alexis Marie Von Furstenburg, Alize', Aloe Vera, Alysin Wonderland, Amanda Bone DeMornay, Amanda Lay, Amanda Roberts, Amy DeMilo, Anastasia Fallon, Angie Ovahness, Anita Mandinite, Appolonia Cruz, Ashlyn Tyler, Aurora Tr'Nele Michelle, Azia Sparks, Barbie Dayne, Barbra Herr, Beverly LaSalle, Bianca DeMonet, Bianca Lynn Breeze, Blair Michaels, Boxxa Vine, Brittany T Moore, Britney Towers, Brandi Amara Skyy, Brooke Lynn Bradshaw, Candi Samples, Candi Stratton, Candy

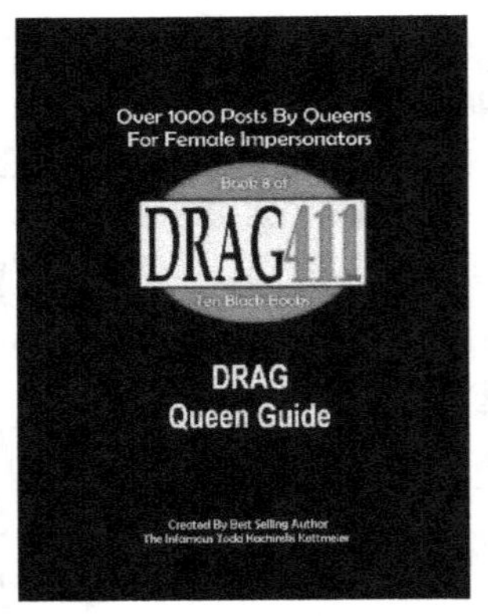

Sugar, Cathy Craig, Catia Lee Love, CeCe Georgia, Cee-Cee LaRouge-Avalon, Celeste Starr, Chad Michaels, Chevon Davis, Cheyenne Desoto Mykels, Chi Chi Lalique, Christina Collins, Chrystal Conners, Claudia B Eautiful, Coca Mesa, Coco St James, Damiana LaRoux, Dana Scrumptious, Danyel Vasquez, Dee Gregory, Delores T. Van-Cartier, Demonica DaBaum, Denise Russell, Diamond Dunhill, Diva Lilo, Diva Savage, Dove, EdriAna Treviño, Elle Emenopé, Elysse Giovanni, Erica James, Esmé Rodríguez, Estella Sweet, Eunyce Raye, Eva Nichole Distruction, Faleasha Savage, Felicia Minor, Felicity Frockaccino, Gigi Masters, Ginger Alley, Ginger Gigi Diamond, Ginger Kaye Belmont, Glitz Glam, Grecia Montes D' Occa, Heather Daniels, Hennessy Heart, Hershae Chocolatae, Holy McGrail, Hope B Childs, Horchata, India Brooks, India Ferrah, Ivy Profen, Izzy Adahl, Jaclyn St James, Jade Iroq, Jade Sotomayor, Jade Taylor Stratton, Jamie-Ree Swan, Jennifer Warner, Jessica Brooks, Jexa Ren'ae Van de Kamp, Joey Brooks, Jonny Pride, Kamelle Toe, Karma Jayde Addams, Kelly Turner, Mama Savannah Georgia, Mr. Kenneth Blake, Kamden T. Rage, Kira Stone-St James, Kirby Kolby, Kita Rose, Krysta Radiance, Lacie Bruce, Lady Jasmine Michaels, Lady Pearl, Lady Sabrina, Latrice Royale, LaTonga Manchez, Leona Barr, Lexi Alexander, Lilo Monroe, Lindsay Carlton, Lucinda Holliday, Lunara Sky, Lupita Chiquita Michaels Alexander, Madam Diva Divine, Mahog Anny, Makayla Michelle Davis Diamond, Mariah Cherry, Maxine Padlock, Melody Mayheim, Menaje E'toi, Mercede Andrews, Mi$hal, Mia Fierce, Michelle Leigh Sterling, Miss Diva Savage, Miss GiGi,

Misty Eyez, Mitze Peterbilt, Monica Mystique, Montrese Lamar Hollar, Morgana DeRaven, Muffy Vanbeaverhousen, Natasha Richards, Nathan Loveland, Nicole Paige Brooks, Nikki Garcia, Nostalgia Todd Ronin, Olivia St James, Paige Sinclair, Pandora DeCeption, Pheobe James, Reia'Cheille Lucious, Robyn Demornay, Robyn Graves, Rhonda Sheer, Rose Murphy, Ruby Diamond NY, Ruby Holiday, Ryan Royale, Rychard "Alpha" Le'Sabre, Rye Seronie, Sable Monay, Sabrina Kayson-Raye, Samantha St Clair, Sanaa Raelynn, Sapphire T. Mylan, Sasha Phillips, Savannah Rivers, Savannah Stevens, Selina Kyle, Sha'day Halston-St James, ShaeShae LaReese, Shamya Banx, Shana Nicole, Shaunna Rai, Sierra Foxx White, Sierra Santana, Sonja Jae Savage, Stella D'oro, Strawberry Whip, Sugarpill, Tasha Carter, Tanna Blake, Taquella Roze, Tawdri Hipburn, Taylor Rockland, Tempest DuJour, Tiffani T. Middlesexx, Traci Russell, Trudy Tyler, Vanessa del Rey, Velveeta WhoreMel, Vera Delmar, Vicky Summers, Vita DeVine, Vivian Sorensin, Vivian Von Brokenhymen, Vivika D'Angelo-Steele, Wendy G. Kennedy, Willmuh Dickfit, Wynter Storm, Yasmine Alexander and ZuZu Bella.

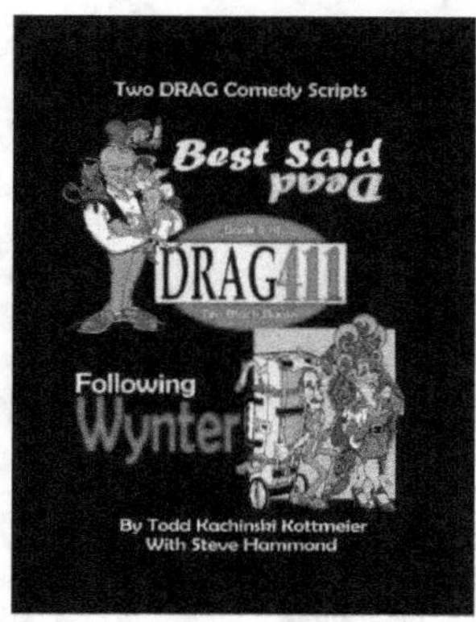

Book 9: DRAG411's (Two Comedy Scripts)
"Best Said Dead" and **"Following Wynter"**

Best Said Dead examines in funny conversations those brief minutes after a person dies. Many religions and beliefs define different paths for each of us. Rarely do we discuss those precious moments between death and the final destination. This comedy opens the possibilities that for a moment, a person vanishes into the memories in their mind. Any part can be male, female, or ambiguous.

Following Wynter is a hilarious comedy play. Ethan discovers his newlywed husband is the flamboyant DRAG queen Wynter Storm in this whimsical farce with an important message of believing in yourself and your friends. . . even if your friend is Serena Silver. Any part can be male, female, or ambiguous.

Book 10:   DRAG411's
"DRAG World"

The contributing writers of DRAG411's "Spotlight Magazine," the World's Largest Paperback Magazine for Impersonators and Fans when it premiered in 2012 with over 175 pages, created this companion book. DRAG411 no longer prints Spotlight Today Magazine, but above you will find Book 7 is the re-release of the groundbreaking first edition. Complete chapters on DRAG Marketing by DRAG411.

Complimentary articles on Confidence, Duct Tape, Music Selection, Living Divinely, authentic stage presence, Pageants, having fun performing, jewelry, legislative information from the United States and around the world, the Old School performers, Virgin stage performers, and payday from contributing writers including Denise Russell, Jay Santana, Chance Wise, Vivikah Kayson-Raye, AJ Menedez, Glenn Storm, Freddy Prinze Charming, Gage Gatlyn, Kevin B. Reed, and over 100 impersonators from around the world!

Other books from the Best Selling author
The Infamous Todd Kachinski Kottmeier

"Turn Around Bright Eyes, The DRAG Queen Killer"

Few crimes in gay history rocked a nation as great as The DRAG Queen Killer. The country seemed paralyzed from the first ring of the chain tapping on the concrete, as they pulled Cassandra to her death, until the very last brutal killing. The murderous rampage seemed buried amongst the media suffering from a barrage of tales from the 9-11 terrorist attacks.

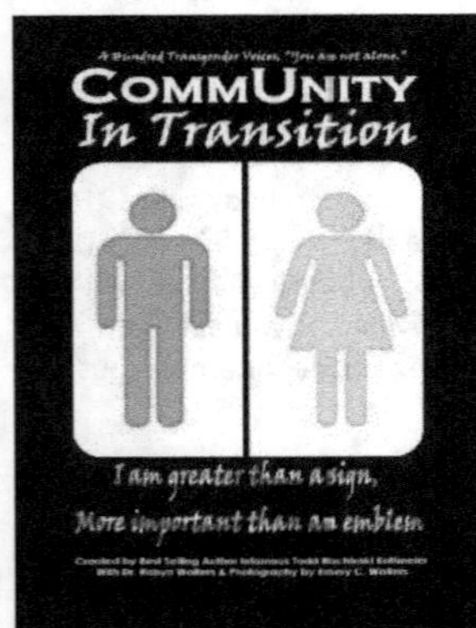

"CommUnity of Transition"

We sent over a thousand invitations to the transgender community around the world asking them to share wisdom, advice, and compassion for those questioning or struggling. No restraints, using topics they created, as they guided the conversation over forty chapters and fifty topics. By the close, these remarkable people had created the largest compilation book in transgender history. They opened their heart with these words.

NOTE: *This book is "lightly edited" to reflect the intent and form of over one hundred transgender contributors. Unedited photographs "before and after" come from actual contributing transgender writers.*

"Joey Brooks, The Show Must Go On"
By Joey Brooks and Todd Kachinski Kottmeier

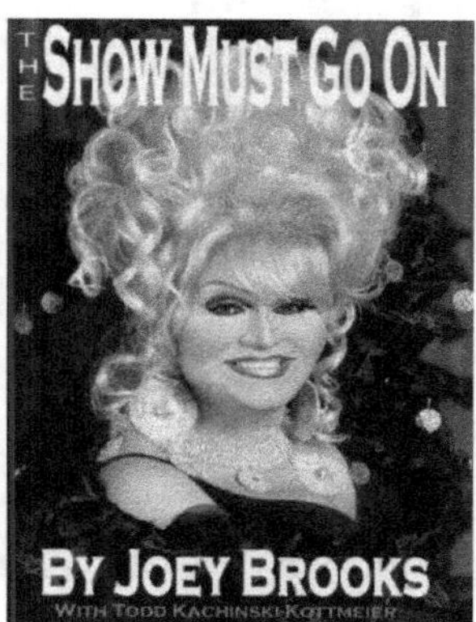

Joey Brooks, The Show Must Go On is the story of The First Lady of Ybor from the days of El Goya to present day. Female Impersonator, Show director, hostess, author… "Old school, new school, no school… who gives a shit? I'm too old to go to school. I barely remember last week. When I get too old to remember what the fuck I did when I was young …ger, I'll just open one of these books and laugh my ass off. I wonder how many other queens had this much fun becoming one of the icons of their community. Too funny. I just called myself an icon. Hell, I must be a queen. Only a female impersonator could call themselves a diva, a queen, a star without people giggling behind her back. Giggling is good. A twenty-dollar bill is better."

"Two Days Past Dead"

The Author's First Published Book

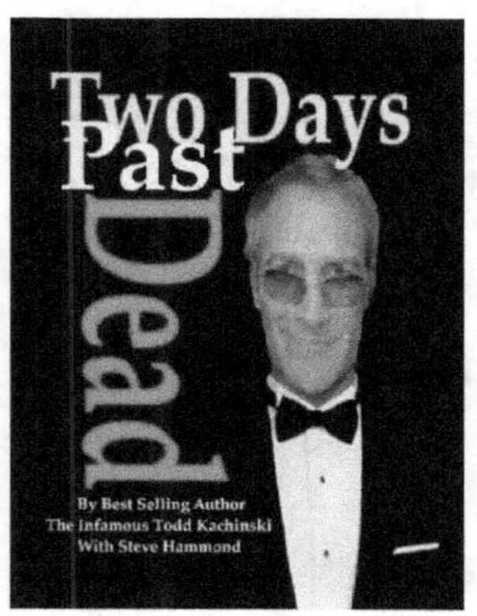

It is hard to be the good guy when you succeed so well being bad. This is the Auggie Summer's dilemma his entire life. The story, based loosely on the tales of The Infamous Todd, follows the precocious child. His story begins with selling candy in 9th grade where he catches not only the attention of the press but also amusement of the drug cartel early in its' own infancy. Auggie Summers finds himself in the forefront of one of the most dangerous organizations on Earth.

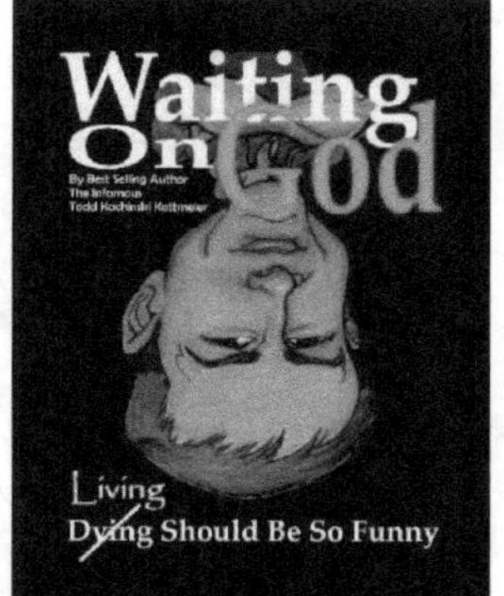

"Waiting On God"
The Author's Humorist Novel

Learn to live after the doctors tell you "that are dying." A humorist essay on embracing funny moments and to create an environment around you that makes people not only laugh, but also be inspired by your strength.

www.ingramcontent.ccm/pod-product-compliance
Lightning Source LLC
Chambersburg PA
CBHW070129260726

48658CB00001B/332